Skills for Success for your second grader

A+ Student

Written by
Annette Taulbee

Illustrations by
Patty McCloskey

Cover Photography by Anthony Nex of Anthony Nex Photography

Photo Credits: © 1997 Comstock, Inc.: pages 1, 3, 7, 8, 16, 28, 33, 35, 36, 38, 45, 47, 48, 51, 54, 55, 57, 58, 59, 64

FS-23003 Skills for Success for Your Second Grader
All rights reserved—Printed in the U.S.A. Copyright © 1997 Frank Schaffer Publications, Inc.

Table of Contents

Introduction

The Sensational Second Grader 1

The Keys to Using This Book 2

Academic Skills

Reading 3–9

Language Arts 10–19

Math 20–31

Science 32–34

Social Studies. 35–37

Art 38–40

Music. 41–43

Physical Education 44–46

Social Skills

Teams and Clubs 47

Getting Along with Siblings 48

Home Responsibilities 49–50

Following Rules 51

Problem Solving. 52–53

Safety 54

Friends 55

Manners 56

Character Development 57–59

Home and School Cooperation

Getting Your Child Organized 60

Homework 61

Volunteering 62

School Events 63

Report Cards and Conferences. 64

Home and School Communication . . 65

TLC for Teachers. 66

Other School Services. 67

Tardies and Absences. 68

Rewards

Bookmark and Badges 69–70

Student Workbook

Skills Worksheets. 71–94

The Sensational
Second Grader!

Parents wear many hats every day. Each one is equally important, but sometimes parents are nervous about wearing the hat of "teacher" for their child. The truth is that all day every day the invisible "teacher hat" is perched on your head, perhaps even on top of another hat you may be wearing at the moment! The joy of parenting comes with making the most of every opportunity to be your child's "teacher."

Parents can be nervous about performing the role of teacher because they are not sure what expectations or goals are realistic for their child at each level. This book is aimed at helping you understand, appreciate, and accentuate the learning that your child is ready to experience.

You were and still are your child's first and most important teacher. By becoming familiar with the skills a second grader needs, you can be more efficient and effective as you continue in that role.

* They are **enthusiastic.** They bubble over with energy in the activities that interest them.

* They are **fascinated** with the world around them.

* They are **friendly.** They like being around people.

* They are **devoted** to their favorite people and projects.

* They are **inquisitive.** They want to know the how and why of things.

* They are **considerate** and recognize when others are not.

* They are **observant.** Their keen eyes and ears may notice things yours do not.

* They are **concerned** with how they do and how they fit in their world.

* They are **radiant** when they accomplish a goal and can share it with others.

* They are **ready to learn and grow** with your direction and the ideas in this book.

The Keys to Using This Book

Be a Learner

Be ready to tell your child that you don't know something. A question from your child indicates interest in the topic, but you don't need to feel embarrassed if you don't know the answer. The important step is to help your child look for an answer.

Teach to the Moment

Remember that the best time to teach anything is the moment your child has expressed curiosity about it. If your child asks a question about the phases of the moon, try to provide information, look it up with him or her in a science book or encyclopedia, and watch the sky. If you have access to the Internet or a computer with a multimedia reference tool, use that to gain instant facts to share.

Teach Academic Skills

The first section of this book provides a guide for you that's full of activities that center around the topics second graders study in school. Use it to help your child better understand a topic that is being taught, and to enhance the learning your child is doing at school. Use the background information and the ideas to provide enjoyable interaction with your child.

Teach Social Skills

The next section centers around social skills. Even the most intelligent child will be less successful in school without good personal skills. These interpersonal skills are critical for positive relationships to develop and for your child to feel worthwhile. Use this section to provide an approach to a problem or an opening to discuss a topic. With prior discussion about these vital skills, your child will have strategies to deal with concerns when they appear.

Promote Home and School Cooperation

The next section of the book gives you practical ideas for how to navigate home and school interaction on a daily basis. There are suggestions for organizing, communicating with the educational community, conferencing with teachers, and getting involved at school.

Give Praise

Included in the book are reward items. Use these to show your child that you are proud of his or her efforts. Children respond to positive reinforcement. Teachers know that the more specific the praise, the better. "Good job!" is great to hear, but more repeat performances come from phrases such as "You wrote your story so neatly that it is easy for me to read. That shows me you are proud of it, too!"

Give Practice

The final section is skill pages for your child that reinforce the activities suggested in the first section. Use them to check on your child's understanding of the skill. Use them to provide individual practice for a skill. Use them to provide a chance for your child to demonstrate progress! If your child has difficulty, you may want to repeat an activity or choose a new approach to help him or her master that skill.

Reading Skills Second Graders Need

PHONICS, VOCABULARY, AND LITERARY SKILLS

Your child will continue learning to recognize the sounds individual letters and combinations make. Second graders often study these concepts and use them to sound out words:

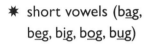

* short vowels (b<u>a</u>g, b<u>e</u>g, b<u>i</u>g, b<u>o</u>g, b<u>u</u>g)

* long vowels (t<u>a</u>pe, <u>e</u>ve, b<u>i</u>ke, r<u>o</u>pe, c<u>u</u>te)

* consonant blends (<u>br</u>own, <u>gl</u>ue, <u>str</u>ike)

* consonant digraphs (<u>sh</u>ip, <u>ch</u>air, <u>th</u>is)

* two-letter regular vowels (m<u>ai</u>l, t<u>ea</u>m, g<u>oa</u>t)

* vowel digraphs (b<u>oo</u>k, br<u>ea</u>k, l<u>aw</u>n)

* r-controlled vowels (h<u>er</u>, c<u>ar</u>, f<u>or</u>, t<u>ur</u>n, p<u>ear</u>)

* diphthongs (<u>oi</u>l, b<u>oy</u>, h<u>ou</u>se, c<u>ow</u>, n<u>ew</u>)

Your child will need to increase his or her reading proficiency throughout the year by continuing to develop vocabulary and fluency in reading grade-level material. Second graders study these areas in vocabulary:

* sight words (words recognized instantly)

* compound words (words made up of two words, such as *bookmark*)

* synonyms (words that mean the same, such as *happy* and *content*)

* antonyms (word opposites, such as *go* and *stop*)

* homophones (words that sound alike but have different spellings and meanings, such as *meat* and *meet*)

Your child will be listening to and reading a variety of different types of literature throughout the year, such as folktales, fairy tales, tall tales, myths, legends, realistic fiction, fantasy, poetry, nonfiction, informational materials, and so on. If your child likes only one type right now, one particular author, or is stuck on dinosaurs, don't be concerned. The important thing is for him or her to be motivated to read!

COMPREHENSION

It is important for your child to read and understand what he or she is reading. Gaining meaning from the written word is the purpose of reading. Fiction, or "make-believe" stories, have basic characteristics that you can help your child begin to identify. Ask the following types of questions as your child reads to you or listens to you read:

* Who is the main character in this story? What is he or she like?

* What is the main character's problem in this story? How does the problem get solved?

* Who are the other characters and what are they like?

* Where and when does the story take place? (setting) Have you ever been to a place like that? Would you like to? Why or why not?

PHONICS

There are some letter sounds your child probably already knows, such as the consonants, and perhaps the short vowel sounds (a, e, i, o, u). Many other phonetic concepts will be presented in second grade. Take your cue as to what to help your child with by looking at the weekly spelling list, homework papers, and daily classwork. Once a concept has been introduced, your child should then begin to use it correctly in writing and when sounding out those words in reading.

BASIC PHONICS RULES

Short vowels—If a word or syllable has one vowel and it comes at the beginning or in between two consonants, the vowel is usually short.

Examples: ant, pet, hit, top, sun

Long vowels—Long vowels say their own name.

1. Silent e Rule—A silent **e** at the end of a word will make the first vowel long.
   Examples: make, eve, like, poke, rude

2. Two-Letter Vowel Rhyme—If two vowels go walking, the first one does the talking.
   Examples: rain, coat, seat, peel

3. Long vowel—If a vowel comes at the end of a word or syllable, it is usually long.
   Examples: no, he, minus

Y as a vowel—As a vowel, *y* usually has a long **i** or long **e** sound. It has a long **i** sound at the end of one-syllable words.

Examples: my, cry, baby, party, cycle

THUMBS UP, THUMBS DOWN

This game can be used with almost any phonics skill. Ask your child to listen for a sound as you say some words, for instance, the short vowel **a**. Your child's thumb goes up if the word contains a short **a** sound, and goes down if the word has any other vowel sound. Give words such as these: *cat, fan, hit, ant, pot, sun, sat,* and *man.*

MAGNET MANIA!

Many toy stores carry inexpensive sets of magnetic letters. If possible, buy the lowercase ones first, since the majority of the words your child reads and writes will be lowercase letters. Use a magnetic board, the refrigerator, or any other magnetic surface in the house. Your child can first practice putting the letters in alphabetical order. Then practice different word families. For example, if long vowel **a** words with a silent **e** at the end are being taught in school, spell out *bake.* Then substitute the first letter with other consonants to make new words for your child to read such as *cake, fake, lake, make, rake, sake, take,* and *wake.* You can also have your child make his or her own words.

PHONICS PICTURE CARDS

Create picture cards to practice phonics concepts. Cut pictures from magazines that match one-syllable words such as *sun, cat, dog, boy, girl, car, boat, plane, tree, house, shoe*. Glue each to a separate index card. Use the cards with the activities that follow.

ABC Order

Give your child a set of 10 cards to put in alphabetical order by the letter(s) of the first sound.

Picture-Word Match-up

Make words using magnetic letters or simply write them in large letters on paper. Have your child find the matching picture card.

Sort Them!

Give your child directives for sorting the cards. For example, pull out all the cards that have a short **i** or long **i** vowel sound. Have your child separate them into short **i** and long **i** piles.

There are many other ways the cards could be sorted—beginning sound, ending sound, short vowel sound, long vowel sound, rhyming words, and so on.

Or, begin with all the cards. Have your child sort them into two groups—words that have a short **a** vowel sound and words that do not.

Memory Match

Play a "Memory" game by pulling out a set of paired cards, such as the short vowel cards. Place them facedown on a table. The first player turns over two cards. If the two pictures match, in this case have the same vowel sound, the player keeps them and takes another turn. If the cards do not match, the player puts them back facedown and the turn is over. Play until all pairs are matched. The player with the most pairs wins.

cat	boat	frog
fire	boot	bat
mouse	coat	wire
dog	root	house

Riddle Me

Choose a dozen cards. Take turns making up a riddle about each card. Examples: This animal is pink and has a short **i** vowel sound (pig). This word rhymes with coat and begins with *b*. (boat)

VOCABULARY

sails
sailed
sailing

Sounding Out New Words

When your child encounters an unknown word, use the following technique to help him or her learn new vocabulary.

1st time: If it is a sound your child has already been taught, say, "What is the beginning sound? What is the ending sound? What is the vowel sound?" After your child gives you the sounds, then you say the word.

2nd time: Say, "Sounds?" After your child gives you the sounds, give the word.

3rd time: Your child will usually give you the sounds, then say the word from memory.

4th time: Your child will say the word!

Your child should use whatever phonics rules have already been taught, but cannot be expected to go beyond that. Be sure to help him or her recognize letters that should be said together when sounding them out. For example, the sound *sh* makes in ship should be sounded out as *sh*, <u>not</u> as an *s* and an *h*.

Word Endings

Sometimes a long word will intimidate your child. If the word has an ending, such as *s*, *ed*, or *ing*, cover the ending with your finger while your child reads the remaining part of the word. Then uncover the ending and focus on it. Next let your child put the two parts together.

Word Card Practice

If your child consistently has trouble with a word, even after the above technique has been used, begin a set of word cards. Any small piece of paper will do or use index cards for a sturdier set. Before your child starts to read, play a game by showing him or her the words one at a time. If your child gets the word correct, give him or her the card. If your child misses it, put the card at the back of the pile to practice again. You can keep the word cards in a box, put a rubber band around them, or hole punch each one in the top left corner and put them on a ring to keep them tidy.

Compound Word Fun

A compound word is made by putting together two words such as *sailboat*. Make a set of word cards that could be mixed and matched to make compound words. Stack the cards and read through them together once. Then spread out the cards faceup. Take turns placing your hands on two cards that together make a compound word.

any	blue	milk	ball
every	berry	star	foot
some	bird	sun	base
where	gold	flash	basket
thing	fish	shine	bare
one	fly	light	night
black	butter	snow	fall

READING TIPS

Practice Makes Perfect

If you want to become a good reader—READ! Children need lots of practice reading. It is important for your child to read at his or her appropriate level. Use the "rule of thumb" described below as a guideline. Then before reading, have your child look at the cover and the pictures. Ask what he or she can tell about the book just by the illustrations. This generates interest and opens up questions about what might happen in the story.

The "Rule of Thumb"

Have your child open to the middle of the book and read a page. Keep track of mistakes on your fingers. If your child misses up to four words, it is still a "thumbs up" book. It is at a level where he or she can understand the content, and be learning new vocabulary. Once a child makes five mistakes, your thumb goes down. The book would be too difficult for your child to read successfully on his or her own. If your child shows interest in a book that is too hard to read independently, you can still get it and read it together or read it to your child!

Five-Middle-Five

A fun activity that encourages your child to read is "Five-Middle-Five." You read aloud the first five pages of the story to help acquaint your child with the characters, plot, and vocabulary. Together read the middle section of the story, making sure to slow your natural pace to help your child read along. Your child reads the last five pages of the story to you.

Visit the Library

The library is full of fascinating materials and costs you nothing! Make friends with the children's librarian. He or she can orient you to specific areas of interest to your child. Most libraries are switching or have switched to a computerized catalog. Ask for assistance if the technology is new to you. Then help your child find books of particular interest or by a special author. A little at a time, your child needs to become familiar with how a library is organized. He or she will need to use it all the way through college!

Books aren't the only materials available for check out. Your library may have magazines, tapes, CDs, videos, and art prints. While you're there, ask about special storytelling times, plays, puppet shows, or summer reading programs. Find a book for yourself, too! It's important for your child to see you reading.

Literature Resources

✱ Jim Trelease's *The New Read-Aloud Handbook* (Penguin, rev. ed. 1995) has outstanding ideas and annotated book lists.

✱ If you have Internet access, try this website: *The Children's Literature Web Guide* http://www.ucalgary.ca/~dkbrown/index.html

MORE READING TIPS

Garage Sale Treasure Hunts

Here is an inexpensive way to add to books you already have at home. Take off early on a Saturday morning for garage sales with your child. You can find books for a dime or a quarter! This is a great activity to get your child motivated to read more.

Reading Rewards

Your child may need some encouragement to read. Help your child keep a record of the books he or she reads and the time spent. For every 100 minutes, reward your child with a book, a frozen yogurt, rental of a special movie, staying up an hour later, a small toy, or some other little prize.

Rereading Favorite Books

If your child wants to read a favorite book over and over again, let him or her! It will help with your child's speed and fluency. Does your child have the book memorized? Ask him or her to start with the last page and read the book backwards! If your child likes that book so much, find other titles by the same author.

Reading is All Around You

Reading should not be limited to books. When you're reading the newspaper, give your child the comics. (Right after you're done with them!) When you're in a restaurant, let your child read the menu. At the market, have him or her read from the cans and boxes on the shelves. In the car, look for signs to read. If you're following a recipe, let your child read it, too. When you assemble a toy, make sure your child participates in reading the directions and following the illustrations. If you watch television, let your child read the program guide to find out when his or her favorite show is on. Your child will begin to see how important reading is in every aspect of our lives.

TV Tip! Reading Rainbow is a great program that reads books to children and also does other terrific activities to go with the stories. Videocassettes of the program may be available through your library or video store.

Record Bedtime Stories

Reading to your child at this age is as important as having your child read. An excellent time to do this is at bedtime. A good technique is to have your child start getting ready for bed at 8:00, with bedtime at 8:30. The faster he or she is, the more time there will be for you to read! If you have a cassette recorder, put it on while you read the story. The book and cassette can then be put in a sealed plastic bag for your child to listen to anytime. These are great to have on a long car trip! Besides, wouldn't you love to have a recorded story that your parents read to you when you were young? These can become real keepsakes!

BOOKS TO READ

Folklore, Tall Tales, Myths

Beauty and the Beast by Jan Brett (Clarion, 1989)

The Chinese Mirror by Mirra Ginsburg (Harcourt Brace Jovanovich, 1988)

Dragonfly's Tale by Kristina Rodanas (Clarion, 1991)

The Gods and Goddesses of Olympus by Aliki (HarperCollins, 1994)

Mufaro's Beautiful Daughters by John Steptoe (Lothrop, Lee & Shepard, 1987)

Pecos Bill by Patsy Jensen (Troll, 1994)

Picture Books

Down By the Bay by Raffi (Crown, 1987)

Happy Birthday, Moon by Frank Asch (Prentice-Hall, 1982)

I Wish I Were a Butterfly by James Howe (Harcourt Brace Jovanovich, 1987)

Ira Sleeps Over by Bernard Waber (Houghton Mifflin, 1972)

Love You Forever by Robert Munsch (Firefly, 1986)

Maria Molina and the Days of the Dead by Kathleen Krull (Macmillan, 1994)

The Patchwork Quilt by Valerie Flournoy (Dial, 1985)

The Polar Express by Chris Van Allsburg (Houghton Mifflin, 1985)

Stellaluna by Janell Cannon (Harcourt Brace, 1993)

The Velveteen Rabbit by Margery Williams (Doubleday, 1958)

Poetry

Beneath a Blue Umbrella by Jack Prelutsky (Greenwillow, 1990)

Falling Up by Shel Silverstein (HarperCollins, 1996)

Pass It On: African-American Poetry for Children selected by Wade Hudson (Scholastic, 1993)

Informational Books

Children Just Like Me by Sue Copsey (Dorling Kindersley, 1995)

Diego by Jeanette Winter (Knopf, 1991) [Spanish/English]

The Magic School Bus Inside the Human Body by Joanna Cole (Scholastic, 1989)

Shapes by Philip Yenawine (Delacorte, 1991)

Easy Reader/Short Chapter Books

Frog and Toad Are Friends by Arnold Lobel (HarperCollins, 1970)

Mr. Putter and Tabby Pour the Tea by Cynthia Rylant (Harcourt Brace, 1994)

Pinky and Rex by James Howe (Atheneum, 1990)

Chapter Books to Read Aloud

The Cuckoo Child by Dick King-Smith (Hyperion, 1993)

Go Fish by Mary Stolz (HarperCollins, 1991)

Mush, a Dog From Space by Daniel Pinkwater (Atheneum, 1995)

Russell and Elisa by Johanna Hurwitz (Morrow, 1989)

Language Arts Skills Second Graders Need

Spelling

Your child will have a spelling program of some kind at school, which may require additional home study. Spelling lists may be organized around specific phonics rules or spelling patterns. In addition, your child needs to spell high frequency words used in daily writing.

Writing

School writing programs encourage children to write using a variety of forms such as a story, letter, journal, report, observation, and poem. Many teachers emphasize a writing process that usually includes these stages:

Pre-writing—thinking of ideas

Rough Draft—writing the first version

Editing—looking for ways to improve the writing (changing words or ideas, checking spelling, punctuation, capitalization, and grammar)

Revising—making corrections

Final Copy—writing a neat, correct final version

Penmanship

Penmanship practice in second grade usually works on mastery of manuscript letters (printing). Check with your child's teacher to see which manuscript style is taught at your school. See page 15 for the two major styles.

Speaking Skills

Second graders learn to speak loudly, clearly, and with expression when speaking to a group. They may participate in choral readings and recite poems, rhymes, and songs. Your child may be asked to present a short talk to the class about a topic. The most common speaking activity is contributing to group discussions.

Listening Skills

Second graders need to listen quietly and attentively when others are speaking. Listening activities within the class may include following oral directions that have three or four steps and answering comprehension questions after listening to a story.

Grammar and Mechanics

Second graders usually work on these skills:

Grammar
* Identify nouns, verbs, and adjectives.

* Use noun-verb agreement. Correct: She walks quickly. Incorrect: She walk quickly.

* Use correct plurals.

Punctuation
* Use ending punctuation of periods, question marks, and exclamation points.

* Use commas in dates and in greetings and closings of friendly letters.

* Use apostrophes in contractions.

Capitalization
* Capitalize the beginning of a sentence, the word *I*, names, titles, dates, holidays, streets, cities, and special things and places.

SPELLING

Your child will probably have a spelling book or spelling program at school. Homework often will be some kind of spelling practice. If your child needs extra practice, try some of these activities to make it more interesting. If your child is given a spelling list on Monday for a test on Friday, don't wait until Thursday night to help your child practice. It is always better to have a few short practice sessions than one long one.

Record It

Have a tape recorder? Record the spelling list for the week on a cassette. Or let your child record it. Then he or she can take a practice test at home! Be sure to give enough time between words for your child to write them. The correct spelling can even be given at the end of the tape for your child to check the words on his or her own. You can record right over these words with next week's lesson.

Rainbow Tracing

Instead of just writing a spelling word three times with a pencil, have your child write a word the first time with a yellow crayon, then go over the word in blue crayon, then in red. The effect will be a colorful rainbow!

Salt Trays

Pour some salt in an old shoebox lid. Give your child a spelling word to print in the salt. After checking it, the word can be erased with a shake of the lid.

Roll, Roll, Roll Your Letters, Gently Into Words!

When particular words keep giving your child trouble, let him or her roll clay into long strips, and then form the letters of the word.

Computer Fun

If you have a computer (or a typewriter), have your child type each word three times or type a sentence for each word.

The Shape I'm In

Have your child write spelling words on the left side of a sheet of graph paper, using one square for short letters (a, o, m) and two squares for tall letters (b, l, t) or tail letters (g, j, p). Next follow the lines to outline each word shape. Draw the matching box shapes on the right side of the paper. Then give a practice test and have your child find the matching box shape and write the word within it.

MORE SPELLING ACTIVITIES

Trace Erase

If you have a small blackboard and chalk, let your child print the spelling list on it. Next have your child trace over each letter with a finger as he or she says it and then pronounce the entire word. The tracing will help your child "imprint" the spelling of the word. It will also erase the word so the activity can be done again!

Add a Letter

This activity gets your child to focus on each letter of a word. Direct your child to write the first letter of the word on the first line, the first and second letter on the second line, and so on. For example, *make* would look like this:

```
m
ma
mak
make
```

Consonants or Vowels?

Be sure your child knows the vowels (*a, e, i, o, u,* and sometimes *y*). Have your child print the spelling words, then trace over the vowels in red crayon. A spelling tip that may help your child is knowing that every syllable has a vowel.

A Spelling Back Rub!

Use your finger to print one of the spelling words on your child's back. Let your child guess which one it is. Switch roles and let him or her spell out one on your back!

Play a Memory Game

Have your child write two sets of spelling words on small pieces of paper. Mix up the pieces and place them facedown. Have one player turn over two words and read them aloud. If they match, the player keeps them and gets another turn. If they do not match, the player puts them back facedown and the turn is over. Take turns and play until all words are matched up. The player with the most pairs wins!

Picture the Word

Spelling requires a visual sense of the word. Good spellers often check a word by writing it a few different ways to find the one that "looks right." Do this activity to help your child develop a mental picture of a word. First let your child study the word by looking at it and spelling it aloud. Then have your child close his or her eyes and picture it. Ask questions such as these to help reinforce the picture:

(Sample word—*stop*)

* What is the first letter? *s*

* What is the last letter? *p*

* What are the tall letters? *t*

* What are the tail letters? *p*

* How many letters are in the word? *4*

* What is the third letter? *o*

* What is the second letter? *t*

* How do you spell the word? *s-t-o-p*

 FS-23003 Skills for Success for Your Second Grader • © Frank Schaffer Publications, Inc.

WRITING

In writing, as well as in reading, encourage your child to use the skills he or she has been taught in school, such as short and long vowels, adding *s*, *ed*, and *ing* to words, and so on. Even adults are not perfect spellers, so it would be unreasonable to expect your second-grade child to spell every word correctly. In a rough draft, your child can use "temporary" or "inventive" spelling, where your child puts down all the letters he or she hears in the word. Let the creativity come first. If a final copy is going to be written, go over the mistakes first, complimenting your child on how close his or her temporary spelling came to the correct spelling of the word. You will find this is an excellent way to make your child apply phonics rules, will free you from having to spell every word for him or her, and give your child confidence in his or her writing ability.

Keep It Simple

Writing can begin with a simple one-sentence caption to go with a picture your child has drawn. Ask your child these questions: *What does a sentence begin with?* (a capital letter) *What does it end with?* (a period) After your child has written the sentence, be sure to have him or her read it back to you. Put it on the refrigerator or other prominent place in the house where it can be shared with other family members and friends. Your child will begin to understand that writing is a way to communicate with others.

Thank You Notes

It's not too soon for your child to start writing thank you notes to grandparents and others for gifts he or she receives. This is a good opportunity to learn the format for friendly letters.

Send Away for Free Goodies!

An extremely motivating letter-writing activity for your child is to send away for free or almost free materials that many companies offer. To find materials you are interested in, look through the most recent version of a book such as *Freebies for Kids and Parents Too* (Probus). Have your child use the letter format on this page. You will need to help with the addressing of the envelope. It will be so exciting for your child to receive something in the mail that he or she will want to write for more!

December 28, 1997

Dear Grandma and Grandpa,
Thank you for the Mancala game you gave me for Christmas. I've already played it three times!
Love,
Danielle

MORE WRITING ACTIVITIES

Pen Pals

Another high-interest letter writing activity is for your child to find a pen pal. Children's magazines are a good source, but simply writing to a cousin or other family member in another state is just as fun. We all love to receive a personal letter in the mail.

If you have Internet access, your child could be an e-mail pen pal with a friend or relative. There are many resources that help children find a pen pal their age, including this one: *International Kids' Space* http://plaza.interport.net/kids_space/

My Trip Journal

During a trip, have your child take some photographs. He or she can write a sentence or two about each day's happenings in a journal (either during the trip or afterwards), then attach a developed photo to each page. This way your child will have a record of your trip.

Tell It to Me First

Sometimes children don't know how to get started on a topic, whether it is writing about a pet, a sports activity, a special friend, a birthday party, or a vacation. Provide time to let your child tell you about the topic. Ask questions and discuss ideas. You may also want to write some of the related vocabulary if your child will need help spelling the words. This technique often helps to get the ball rolling and your child busy writing.

A Handy Plan

Here's an idea for organizing thoughts. Tell your child to trace his or her hand on paper. Have your child write the main topic on the palm and a detail on each finger. Your child can then develop the ideas into sentences or paragraphs. (See page 77 for a sample.)

Writing "Make-Believe" Stories

Second graders are learning to write stories with a beginning, a middle, and an end. It is valuable for your child to plan a story before he or she begins writing it. (Otherwise the story may go on and on and on and still not get anywhere!) Page 78 is a story map to help your child organize thoughts. (You may want to make copies of the page to reuse it.) Talk through the steps together and let your child fill in the map. Then encourage your child to write the story.

Save Original Creations!

Let your child keep his or her best writing in a special folder. Date everything so you can see the growth as it occurs. If you have a tape recorder, have your child record the stories on a cassette to listen to later. As more stories are written, more can be added onto the cassette. This can become a special keepsake.

MANUSCRIPT ALPHABET

Aa Bb Cc Dd Ee Ff Gg

Hh Ii Jj Kk Ll Mm Nn

Oo Pp Qq Rr Ss Tt Uu

Vv Ww Xx Yy Zz

MODERN MANUSCRIPT ALPHABET

Aa Bb Cc Dd Ee Ff Gg

Hh Ii Jj Kk Ll Mm Nn

Oo Pp Qq Rr Ss Tt Uu

Vv Ww Xx Yy Zz

GRAMMAR AND MECHANICS

Parts-of-Speech Pantomime

Play a family pantomime game to practice parts of speech commonly taught in second grade—nouns, verbs, and adjectives. Find three colors of paper. On slips of one color, have family members write nouns that could be acted out (dog, ocean, circle); on slips of another color write verbs (sleep, hop); and on the third color write adjectives (scared, happy). Place the slips in a bowl and take turns picking one and acting it out while the rest of the family guesses.

Speak Correctly

Before children can write correctly, they need to speak correctly. If you hear your child using incorrect grammar, gently guide him or her in repeating the phrase correctly.

What Mark Does It End With?

Teach or review these guidelines for sentence punctuation:

* If a sentence tells you something, it ends with a period. *I like dogs.*

* If a sentence asks you something, it ends with a question mark. *Do you like dogs?*

* If a sentence shows anger, excitement, or surprise, it ends with an exclamation point. *Our dog just had puppies!*

Give your child sentences and have him or her name the end punctuation. Make sure to let your child test you with some sentences, too.

Commas

Many second graders are taught how to use commas within the format of a friendly letter.

In dates: *March 16, 1998*

In the greeting: *Dear Grandpa,*

In the closing: *Yours truly,*

In addresses: *Philadelphia, PA*

Model for your child how to write a friendly letter, pointing out the commas. Then have your child practice by writing a letter to a friend.

Names and Titles Need Capitals

Have your child print a list of everyone's name in your immediate family, pets included, and then some relatives' names, too. People's titles can be discussed also. Point out that boys and men can use the title *Mr.* (Mr. Weber), married women can use the titles *Ms.* or *Mrs.* (Ms. Fox-Weber), and unmarried girls and women can use the titles *Ms.* or *Miss* (Miss Weber).

Grandma Fox
Linda Fox-Weber
Grandma Weber
Andrea Weber
Grandpa Weber
Michael Weber
Uncle Max
Fluffy
Aunt Gloria

MORE CAPITALIZATION IDEAS

Days and Months Need Capitals

Have your child use a calendar to make a list of days of the week and months of the year, being sure to begin each with a capital letter. Have your child practice reading and saying the days of the week and months of the year in order. You may also want to teach abbreviations. Write an abbreviation such as *Tues.* or *Dec.* Point out that each begins with a capital letter and ends with a period. Have your child identify the day or month each abbreviation represents.

Capitals for Special Things

Teach your child that names of special things begin with capital letters. Have your child make a list of toys and games in your home and capitalize them as needed. Together note how capitals are used in titles of books. Check newspaper movie listings, having your child highlight the words that have capitals. When you take your child food shopping, have him or her point out the capitals for brand names.

Capitals for Special Places

Ask your child the following questions, printing the responses so he or she can see how capital letters are used for special places:

* What is the name of your school?
* Where do we go food shopping?
* What river, lake, or ocean is near us?
* What is one mountain you know?
* What is a zoo or museum you like?
* What is your favorite amusement park?

My Street, City, and State

All children at this age should know their address and phone number. Once your child can recite your address, write it down for him or her to read and then copy several times. Show your child return address labels you use, how to address an envelope correctly, and what incoming mail looks like. Point out the use of capitals. When your child writes a letter, help him or her to address the envelope correctly.

Julio Sanchez
1348 Oak Ave.
Denver, CO 81460

Jose Muñoz
643 Seventh Street
Los Angeles, CA 90375

Holidays Need Capitals

For more practice, have your child write each month and list holidays that occur within it. Check published calendars for holidays!

SPEAKING SKILLS

Class Sharing Time

Most students in second grade will still have a sharing time. Many teachers assign a given day for a certain group of students. If so, put it on your calendar to help your child remember. Let your child choose some special things to share. Have him or her practice in front of you the night before using the following format:

I have two things to tell you about my _____. The first thing is _____. The second thing is_____. Does anyone have a question?

Puppet Play

Even shy children come alive when you put puppets on their hands. Keep your eyes open at garage sales and swap meets for inexpensive second-hand ones. You can make simple puppets out of paper bags or socks, or you can cut characters out of construction paper to glue onto wooden sticks. Let your child make up his or her own story to act out.

Reading to Others

Reading out loud to a younger sibling will give your child the opportunity to speak clearly, loudly, and with good expression. Model good oral reading habits to your child, even trying some voice changes for different characters.

Lip Sync

A good confidence builder is to have your child lip sync a song he or she enjoys. Use a play microphone and dress-up clothes for a family performance!

Poetry

As you read Mother Goose and other poetry, such as Shel Silverstein's *Where The Sidewalk Ends*, your child will begin to hear the rhythmic patterns and want to duplicate them. Encourage your child to memorize favorite poems to recite to others! Suggest some simple acting techniques to spice them up.

Plays

There are many simple plays that children can do with other friends. Check at the library and ask your child's teacher for suggestions. Or, just encourage the children to act out a favorite folktale or picture book story.

Record It!

Using a cassette or video recorder, put your child on tape doing any of the suggested activities on this page. He or she can then listen to or watch the results! Both ways of recording are powerful motivators for your child to improve speech techniques.

LISTENING SKILLS

Clap a Pattern

Clap a pattern several times until your child can join in and duplicate it. Then switch to a new pattern. Can your child do it with his or her eyes closed? Be sure to give your child a turn to make up the patterns.

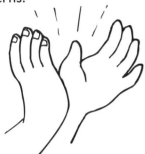

Giving Directions

Teach your child to follow the directions you give. Start with just one direction. Set your child up for success by saying, "Amanda, I am going to give you one direction and you need to repeat it back to me." After she repeats it, compliment her for being a good listener and again when she has followed the direction. Once your child can follow one direction, give two. You may want her to repeat them if you find she has difficulty remembering. Again, compliment her when she is done. Go to three directions when your child has demonstrated she can do two. More than three is too many!

Draw What You Hear

Give your child a piece of drawing paper and crayons or markers. Make up a story. As you narrate it, have your child draw what he or she hears. Add more and more difficult directions that your child needs to follow. Be creative! Example: *Once upon a time there lived a little boy.* (Child draws the boy.) *He lived in a big red house.* (Child draws a red house.) *The house had tiny yellow windows and a blue door.* (Child continues to add details to the picture.)

Close Your Eyes!

This is a fun listening game. Have your child close his or her eyes. No peeking! Use different household items to make sounds and have your child identify them—water running, door closing, silverware rattling, wax paper being torn, microwave going on. You've got the idea!

Story Comprehension

As you read to your child, ask questions about the story. At the end, have your child retell the story in his or her own words. This will let you know how well your child understood the story.

Interrupting Adult Conversations

When two people are talking and you want to say something, how do you know when to break into the conversation? You must listen and at an appropriate time begin speaking, or say, "Excuse me." Children must be taught this skill or they will constantly interrupt you. Help them practice. If they start to break in at the wrong time, let them know you will put your hand up to indicate they are to stop and wait. Teach them to say, "Excuse me." Be sure to compliment them for being polite and waiting patiently when they do so.

Math Skills
Second Graders Need

In second grade, your child will be extending and expanding what he or she learned in math in first grade. Remember, it is not your responsibility to teach these concepts to your child. That is what the teacher has been trained to do. The most helpful thing you can do for the teacher and for your child is to reinforce and enrich each concept that is being taught at school. Keep your eye on classwork as it comes home. It will be your best clue as to what is going on in the classroom.

Addition and Subtraction

Basic Facts—Your child will move from addition and subtraction facts up to 10 (Examples: $5 + 4 = 9$, $10 - 2 = 8$) to the number facts up to 18 (Examples: $7 + 5 = 12$, $18 - 9 = 9$). These addition and subtraction problems are known as "basic facts" because with them your child has the foundation to solve any addition or subtraction problem.

There are two important concepts that will help your child understand the addition and subtraction facts and cut in half the number of facts to be memorized!

1. When adding any two numbers, you can reverse their order and still get the same sum (total). These are known as related facts. Examples:

$2 + 3 = 5$ $8 + 6 = 14$
$3 + 2 = 5$ $6 + 8 = 14$

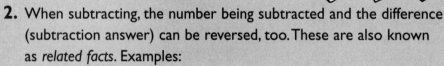

2. When subtracting, the number being subtracted and the difference (subtraction answer) can be reversed, too. These are also known as *related facts*. Examples:

$5 - 2 = 3$ $14 - 8 = 6$
$5 - 3 = 2$ $14 - 6 = 8$

A *fact family* is a set of related facts. Example:

$1 + 9 = 10$

$9 + 1 = 10$

$10 - 1 = 9$

$10 - 9 = 1$

Place Value

The term place value refers to understanding that where a numeral is in a number determines what it is worth.

hundreds   tens   ones
place   place   place

736

7 hundreds   3 tens   6 ones
700   30   6

Here are some place value and counting concepts second graders are expected to master:

✳ Count and write numbers to 1,000.

✳ Skip count by twos, fives, and tens to 100.

✳ Compare two numbers using terms such as: greater than (>), less than (<), and equals (=).

✳ Identify odd (1, 3, 5, 7, 9 . . .) and even (2, 4, 6, 8 . . .) numbers.

5, 10, 15
20, 25

MORE MATH CONCEPTS

Addition and Subtraction

Here are other concepts second graders learn:

✳ Adding three or more numbers

✳ Adding two-digit numbers without regrouping (Don't let the new terms confuse you. Regrouping in addition is what you learned as "carrying.")

Example:
$$\begin{array}{r} 42 \\ + 56 \\ \hline 98 \end{array}$$

✳ Adding two-digit numbers with regrouping (Regrouping is necessary when a column adds up to 10 or more.)

Example:
$$\begin{array}{r} 4\overset{1}{8} \\ + 35 \\ \hline 83 \end{array}$$

✳ Subtracting two-digit numbers without regrouping (Regrouping in subtraction is what you learned as "borrowing.")

Example:
$$\begin{array}{r} 98 \\ - 42 \\ \hline 56 \end{array}$$

✳ Subtracting two-digit numbers with regrouping

Example:
$$\begin{array}{r} \overset{7}{\cancel{8}}\overset{1}{3} \\ - 48 \\ \hline 35 \end{array}$$

Measurement

Second graders learn to measure length, perimeter, weight or mass, and capacity of objects using both customary units (inches; ounces and pounds; cups, quarts, and gallons) and metric units (centimeters; grams and kilograms; milliliters and liters). Children are expected to use and understand both systems of measurement, but <u>are</u> <u>not</u> expected to convert between the two. Second graders also learn to read temperatures on a thermometer.

Time

Your child will review telling time to the hour and half-hour, then move on to minutes. Reading and using a calendar will be covered, too.

Money

Second graders learn the value of pennies, nickels, dimes, quarters, half-dollars, and dollars.

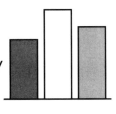

Geometry

Second graders learn about two-dimensional shapes, such as circles, squares, triangles, and rectangles, and three-dimensional figures, such as cubes, cones, and spheres.

Fractions

Second graders learn to identify fractional parts of a shape or group, including halves, thirds, and fourths. They learn the bottom number in a fraction (denominator) tells how many equal parts make up the whole and the top number (numerator) tells how many parts you have.

Graphs

In second grade, your child will enjoy learning how to make and read different kinds of graphs.

Problem Solving

Throughout the year your child will encounter word problems. Second graders learn different strategies for solving a problem—draw a picture, find a pattern, write an addition or subtraction sentence, act it out, use manipulatives, and guess and test.

Other Topics

Your child may also study estimation, mental math, using calculators, probability, patterns, and logical reasoning. Multiplication readiness may be introduced; but third grade is usually when multiplication is emphasized.

PLACE VALUE AND NUMBER SENSE

Odd and Even Numbers

Use any available counters. Small candies like M&M's™ make this even more interesting! Show your child two candies and ask him or her to divide them evenly between the two of you. Tell your child that two is an *even number* because it can be divided evenly, so both people get the same amount. Do the same with 4, 6, 8, and 10 candies. Write down all of the even numbers. Now go back and try the same activity with 1, 3, 5, 7, and 9 candies. Point out that these numbers can't be divided equally so we call them *odd numbers*. Any number ending with 0, 2, 4, 6, or 8 will be even, such as 32, 474, and 1,000. Any number ending with 1, 3, 5, 7, or 9 will be odd, such as 31, 475, and 829.

Is it an odd number?

Is it less than 50?

Guess My Number

This is a fun game to play when in the car or waiting in line. One family member picks a number between 1 and 100. The rest of the family asks questions that can be answered *yes* or *no* to figure out the number.

Tens and Ones

An excellent way for your child to learn about sets of tens and ones is to use pennies and dimes. Have your child count out ten pennies, then trade him or her one dime for the ten pennies. Now your child has one set of ten.

Lowest Number Wins

Write the digits 0 to 9 on separate index cards. Mix up the cards and place them facedown. Take turns picking two cards each and arranging them to make a number. The person with the lowest number wins a point. Then mix up the cards and play again. The first player to score 10 points wins. If your child is ready to read larger numbers, make two sets of cards and let everyone pick three or four cards each.

Roll Out the Dough!

To play this game you will need a pair of dice, some dimes, and some pennies. Let one die represent tens and the other die ones. Each player rolls the tens die and counts out the matching number of dimes, rolls the ones die and counts out the matching number of pennies, and then counts out the total amount, starting with dimes. Compare totals to find who has the most. That player gets a point. The first player to get 10 points wins!

ADDITION FACTS—0 TO 18

0 + 0 = 0	0 + 7 = 7	1 + 9 = 10	4 + 9 = 13
0 + 1 = 1	1 + 6 = 7	2 + 8 = 10	5 + 8 = 13
1 + 0 = 1	2 + 5 = 7	3 + 7 = 10	6 + 7 = 13
0 + 2 = 2	3 + 4 = 7	4 + 6 = 10	7 + 6 = 13
1 + 1 = 2	4 + 3 = 7	5 + 5 = 10	8 + 5 = 13
2 + 0 = 2	5 + 2 = 7	6 + 4 = 10	9 + 4 = 13
	6 + 1 = 7	7 + 3 = 10	
0 + 3 = 3	7 + 0 = 7	8 + 2 = 10	5 + 9 = 14
1 + 2 = 3		9 + 1 = 10	6 + 8 = 14
2 + 1 = 3	0 + 8 = 8		7 + 7 = 14
3 + 0 = 3	1 + 7 = 8	2 + 9 = 11	8 + 6 = 14
	2 + 6 = 8	3 + 8 = 11	9 + 5 = 14
0 + 4 = 4	3 + 5 = 8	4 + 7 = 11	
1 + 3 = 4	4 + 4 = 8	5 + 6 = 11	6 + 9 = 15
2 + 2 = 4	5 + 3 = 8	6 + 5 = 11	7 + 8 = 15
3 + 1 = 4	6 + 2 = 8	7 + 4 = 11	8 + 7 = 15
4 + 0 = 4	7 + 1 = 8	8 + 3 = 11	9 + 6 = 15
	8 + 0 = 8	9 + 2 = 11	
0 + 5 = 5			7 + 9 = 16
1 + 4 = 5	0 + 9 = 9	3 + 9 = 12	8 + 8 = 16
2 + 3 = 5	1 + 8 = 9	4 + 8 = 12	9 + 7 = 16
3 + 2 = 5	2 + 7 = 9	5 + 7 = 12	
4 + 1 = 5	3 + 6 = 9	6 + 6 = 12	8 + 9 = 17
5 + 0 = 5	4 + 5 = 9	7 + 5 = 12	9 + 8 = 17
	5 + 4 = 9	8 + 4 = 12	
0 + 6 = 6	6 + 3 = 9	9 + 3 = 12	9 + 9 = 18
1 + 5 = 6	7 + 2 = 9		
2 + 4 = 6	8 + 1 = 9		
3 + 3 = 6	9 + 0 = 9		
4 + 2 = 6			
5 + 1 = 6			
6 + 0 = 6			

SUBTRACTION FACTS—0 TO 18

0 – 0 = 0	6 – 6 = 0	9 – 9 = 0	12 – 9 = 3
1 – 1 = 0	6 – 5 = 1	9 – 8 = 1	12 – 8 = 4
1 – 0 = 1	6 – 4 = 2	9 – 7 = 2	12 – 7 = 5
2 – 2 = 0	6 – 3 = 3	9 – 6 = 3	12 – 6 = 6
2 – 1 = 1	6 – 2 = 4	9 – 5 = 4	12 – 5 = 7
2 – 0 = 2	6 – 1 = 5	9 – 4 = 5	12 – 4 = 8
3 – 3 = 0	6 – 0 = 6	9 – 3 = 6	12 – 3 = 9
3 – 2 = 1	7 – 7 = 0	9 – 2 = 7	13 – 9 = 4
3 – 1 = 2	7 – 6 = 1	9 – 1 = 8	13 – 8 = 5
3 – 0 = 3	7 – 5 = 2	9 – 0 = 9	13 – 7 = 6
4 – 4 = 0	7 – 4 = 3	10 – 9 = 1	13 – 6 = 7
4 – 3 = 1	7 – 3 = 4	10 – 8 = 2	13 – 5 = 8
4 – 2 = 2	7 – 2 = 5	10 – 7 = 3	13 – 4 = 9
4 – 1 = 3	7 – 1 = 6	10 – 6 = 4	14 – 9 = 5
4 – 0 = 4	7 – 0 = 7	10 – 5 = 5	14 – 8 = 6
5 – 5 = 0	8 – 8 = 0	10 – 4 = 6	14 – 7 = 7
5 – 4 = 1	8 – 7 = 1	10 – 3 = 7	14 – 6 = 8
5 – 3 = 2	8 – 6 = 2	10 – 2 = 8	14 – 5 = 9
5 – 2 = 3	8 – 5 = 3	10 – 1 = 9	15 – 9 = 6
5 – 1 = 4	8 – 4 = 4	11 – 9 = 2	15 – 8 = 7
5 – 0 = 5	8 – 3 = 5	11 – 8 = 3	15 – 7 = 8
	8 – 2 = 6	11 – 7 = 4	15 – 6 = 9
	8 – 1 = 7	11 – 6 = 5	16 – 9 = 7
	8 – 0 = 8	11 – 5 = 6	16 – 8 = 8
		11 – 4 = 7	16 – 7 = 9
		11 – 3 = 8	17 – 9 = 8
		11 – 2 = 9	17 – 8 = 9
			18 – 9 = 9

FS-23003 Skills for Success for Your Second Grader • © Frank Schaffer Publications, Inc.

ADDITION ACTIVITIES AND REGROUPING

Understanding Addition

Find something in the house that can be used for counters, such as beans, pennies, or checker pieces. Use the following steps to teach your child the concept that you can change the order of any two sets (groups of objects) and the sum (total) remains the same.

Show me a set of 3 checkers.

Show me another set of 2 checkers.

How many do you have in all? (5)

Now put the set of 2 checkers first.

Put the set of 3 checkers next to it.

Now how many do you have in all? (5)

Make it a game and ask your child to switch the two sets again and tell how many in all. Ask how that could be. (Play dumb!) Help your child discover how this works, then try it with other combinations that equal 5 (1 + 4, 4 + 1).

Addition With Regrouping ("Carrying")

The best way to help your child when he or she begins this concept in math is to teach your child to talk through the problem. Using the following problem as an example, try these steps with your child:

Where do you always start? (ones)

What does the ones column say to you? (six plus eight)

How much is 6 + 8? (14)

Is there a set of ten in 14? (yes)

[This is where your work with dimes and pennies will help you.]

Would there be any ones left over? (yes)

How many? (4)

Where do you write that number? (in the ones column)

What do you do with the set of ten? (put it in the tens column)

How many tens do you have in all? (8)

How did you figure out how many tens you have? (I added 1 + 4 + 3)

tens	ones	
		1
4	6	46
+ 3	8	+ 38
		84

Slowly, but surely, your child will begin to do this self talk on his or her own. If your child asks, "Do I have to regroup?" he or she does not understand the concept and needs to be guided again through the problem. This is not easy. Be patient.

SUBTRACTION AND REGROUPING

Understanding Subtraction

Use a plastic container and some counters to play "What's Missing?" Start with any given number of objects on top of the container or on a table. Tell your child to close his or her eyes. Slip some of the objects under the container or into one of your hands. Then have your child figure out how many objects are missing. For example, you may start with 12 pennies, slip 7 under the container, leaving 5 on top. Your child must then figure out how many are under the container.

Help your child discover the relationship between two sets in subtraction: Regardless of which set you take away from the total, the other set will always be left.

Example: 12 – 7 = 5, 12 – 5 = 7

Subtraction With Regrouping ("Borrowing")

Ask your child what you do when you are baking cookies and you don't have enough sugar. (You borrow some from a neighbor.) Hand your child a dime. Ask him or her to give you three cents out of it. If your child is stumped, ask what the problem is and how it could be solved. (The dime could be traded for ten pennies, then the three given to you.) That idea will help as you talk your child through solving the following problem that involves "borrowing."

Where do you always start? (ones)

What does the ones column say to you? (2 take away 5)

Can you have 2 ones and take 5 away? (no)

So how do you solve that problem? (borrow from the tens column)

If there are 7 tens and you borrow 1 ten, how many will be left? (6)

How will you show that? (cross out the 7 and put 6 above it)

If you take those 10 ones and add them to the 2 ones you already have, how many ones will you have? (12)

How can you show that? (put a 1 by the 2 to make it 12)

Now what does the ones column say? (12 minus 5, which is 7)

What does the tens column say now? (6 tens take away 3 tens, which is 3 tens)

So what is your answer? (37)

$$\begin{array}{cc} \text{tens} & \text{ones} \\ 7 & 2 \\ - 3 & 5 \end{array} \qquad \begin{array}{r} {}^{6}\!\!\!\not7{}^{1}2 \\ -35 \\ \hline 37 \end{array}$$

This is not an easy concept to learn, and it takes awhile to "cement" it. When your child gets confused, go back and talk through it.

MATH FUN AND TELLING TIME

Telling Time

If you don't have a play clock, make one out of two paper plates. Cut apart one plate to make a short hour hand and a longer minute hand. Use a brad to attach the hour and minute hands to the other plate. Have your child write the clock numbers, beginning with 12, 3, 6, and 9, and then filling in the remaining numbers in the spaces.

Review telling time by the hour and half-hour. Five-minute increments are more difficult. Show your child how to count by fives as he or she moves around the numbers on the clock. Work with times up to 30 minutes first, showing your child the position of the hands on the clock and having him or her tell you the time. Then have your child write the corresponding digital time.

During the day, ask your child to read the time on household clocks. A good incentive for practicing is to tell your child you will buy him or her a watch when he or she can tell time well!

Math Fact Fun

Your child will need to practice the addition or subtraction facts to memorize them. If possible, practice 10 minutes a day. There are many ways to do it:

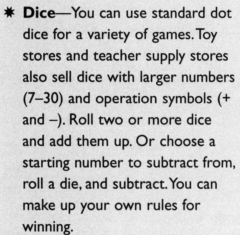

* **Flash Cards**—You can buy a set of cards or make your own. Give your child 10 cards to work on. Hold up a card. If your child can answer it within 5 seconds, he or she keeps the card. If not, you keep it. Play until your child has all 10 cards.

* **Dice**—You can use standard dot dice for a variety of games. Toy stores and teacher supply stores also sell dice with larger numbers (7–30) and operation symbols (+ and –). Roll two or more dice and add them up. Or choose a starting number to subtract from, roll a die, and subtract. You can make up your own rules for winning.

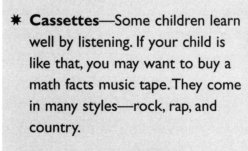

* **Cassettes**—Some children learn well by listening. If your child is like that, you may want to buy a math facts music tape. They come in many styles—rock, rap, and country.

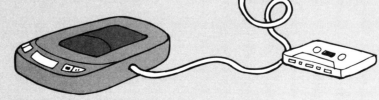

MEASUREMENT

Liquid Measurement

The kitchen is full of things your child can use for liquid measurement. Your child can explore over the sink or outside to see how many cups it takes to fill pint, quart, and gallon containers. Let your child help in baking to show him or her how this skill can be used.

Measuring Length

Your child will need a ruler to learn how to measure the length and height of objects. If possible, buy one with both inch and centimeter markings. Be sure your child lines up the end of the ruler with the end of the object to be measured. When your child is adept at small items, teach him or her how to measure items that are longer than the length of the ruler. Then send your child on a measuring hunt to find these things:

Customary Units Hunt

* three objects that are less than 3 inches long

* three objects that are about 6 inches long

* three objects that are about 12 inches (1 foot) long

* an object that is more than 12 inches (1 foot) long

Metric Units Hunt

* three objects that are less than 1 centimeter long

* three objects that are about 5 centimeters long

* three objects that are about 30 centimeters long

* an object that is about 100 centimeters (1 meter) long

Reading a Time Schedule

If your family watches television, teach your child how to read the program guide. Ask questions such as these:

* What is on at 7:00 tonight?

* What time does your favorite program start?

* How long does it last?

MONEY

Counting Change

Learning how to count out change is difficult for children at this age, but you can try simple problems, teaching your child to count on from the price to the amount given. Start by having your child use only pennies and dimes to give change. For example, pretend you are buying a stuffed animal from your child for 56¢ and you pay with a $1 bill. Your child would count up and say, "Here's your change— 57¢, 58¢, 59¢, 60¢, 70¢, 80¢, 90¢, $1.00."

Money, Money, Money

Be sure your child can identify the name and amount each coin or bill is worth (penny, nickel, dime, quarter, half-dollar, dollar). Double-check your child's ability to count by fives and tens, using nickels and dimes. Teach your child how to skip count using quarters (25¢, 50¢, 75¢, $1.00, $1.25, $1.50, $1.75, $2.00).

There are two basic ways to practice money:

1. Put specific coins on the table and ask your child to "sort, touch, and count." Have your child sort the coins by type and arrange them in lines beginning with the coin worth the most. Next, have your child touch each coin as he or she counts it. For example, if your child arranged a pile of coins into rows of 2 quarters, 3 dimes, 1 nickel, and 4 pennies, he or she would touch each one and say, "Twenty-five, fifty, sixty, seventy, eighty, eighty-five, eighty-six, eighty-seven, eighty-eight, eighty-nine."

2. Ask your child to show you a certain amount of money such as 62¢. Let your child find more than one way of showing the amount. Then challenge him or her to find the way that uses the fewest amount of coins.

Earning money and spending money will give your child the motivation to really learn how to use it. Playing games like *Monopoly* will increase your child's ability to count and use money also.

GEOMETRY, FRACTIONS

Word Problems

When encountering a word problem, your child needs to follow steps similar to these:

1. **Read the problem.** Think about what you know and what you want to find out.

2. **Plan how to solve it.**
   Could you draw a picture? Could you act it out using objects?
   Could you write an addition sentence?
   Could you write a subtraction sentence?
   Could you find a pattern?
   Could you guess and test?

3. **Solve the problem.** Write the answer.

4. **Think about your answer.** Reread the problem. Does your answer make sense?

Geometry

Use clay or play dough to explore shapes. Begin with snakes and use them to make circles, triangles, squares, and rectangles. Then shape mounds to make 3-D figures, such as a sphere, cube, rectangular prism, cylinder, and cone. Look around for real-life examples of the shapes (Earth, bouillon cube, shoebox, can, ice-cream cone).

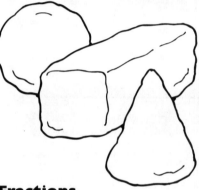

Fractions

You've ordered pizza for dinner. How many equal pieces are there? You are baking and the recipe asks for a half-cup of margarine, one-third cup of milk, and one-fourth cup of nuts. Which measuring cups do you use for each? There are six biscuits left and three people. How many should each person get? These questions and other everyday examples will help your child understand the real-life application of fractions.

PRACTICE WITH PROBLEM SOLVING

Sometimes certain words will give your child a clue as to whether he or she needs to add or subtract.

Addition: How many in all? How many altogether?

Subtraction: How many are left? How many more are needed? How much longer? How much younger?

Here are word problems second graders might encounter:

For many word problems, your child will write a number sentence. He or she needs to read or listen carefully to a problem to decide if things are coming together (addition), going apart (subtraction), or being compared (addition or subtraction).

There are 21 birds on the fence.
Five more birds come.
How many birds are there in all?

Solution: 2 1
          + 5
          ———
           2 6   26 birds

There are 12 birds on the fence.
Three fly away.
How many are left?

Solution: 12 − 3 = 9

9 birds

David is 9 years old.
His brother John is 7.
How much older is David than John?

Solution: 9 − 7 = 2
David is two years older.

Kayla's frog jumped 8 cm (centimeters).
Ebony's frog jumped 5 cm farther than Kayla's.
How far did Ebony's frog jump?

Solution: 8 + 5 = 13

It jumped 13 cm.

Andrew is planting 12 flowers.
He wants this pattern: 2 reds, 1 yellow, 2 reds, 1 yellow . . .
How many red flowers does he need?

Solution: (Draw the pattern.) 8 red flowers

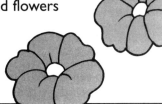

Sarah has four coins that together equal 30¢.
What coins does she have?

Solution: (Guess and test.) 2 dimes and 2 nickels

Science Skills Second Graders Need

Your child's teacher may have a state science framework to follow, as well as some specific district guidelines. The three main science areas taught are Life Science, Earth Science, and Physical Science. There are some basic science skills your child will learn, regardless of which science topics the teacher chooses—predicting, observing and describing, comparing and contrasting, measuring, sequencing, finding cause and effect relationships, recording data, inferring, and drawing conclusions. Keep these in mind as you do science projects at home also.

Here are some science topics commonly taught in second grade. The list does not include everything that could be taught. It is also not possible for a class to study all of the topics in-depth in one school year. When you build on what your child is learning at school, you will enrich and reinforce the concepts.

Life Science

* Study and compare living and nonliving things

* Talk about dinosaurs and the Earth's changes

* Name the parts of a plant and describe their functions

* List the characteristics of different animals

* Describe conditions and materials needed for animals to grow and survive

Physical Science

* Identify characteristics of solids, liquids, and gases

* Find examples of gravity

* Use simple machines

* Discuss how objects expand when heated

* Measure and compare temperature

* Name several sources of light

* Study how a shadow is made

* Discuss how sound is made

* Describe what magnets attract

* Discuss uses of electricity

Earth Science

* Study the sun, the moon, and the planets

* Classify rocks

* Study volcanoes and earthquakes

* Study clouds, rain, snow, and wind

* Explain the water cycle

* Study the sea and its contents

Make an Explorer's Kit

Most children love science. They are curious about the world around them and want to go exploring. Make a kit for your child with items that will help:

* a small notebook (for recording observations or discoveries)

* pencil

* colored pencils, markers, or crayons

* ruler

* magnifying lens

* magnet

* a library card (for checking out books to learn more)

To get started, have your child fill out the beginning sections of page 90. Then encourage him or her to discover more.

SCIENCE ACTIVITIES

Life Science

Take a Hike!—Take a nature hike. If you can, visit your city park and have your child collect samples of living and nonliving things. This will enhance your child's ability to observe the world in which we all live. Encourage your child to describe different objects, including their color, size, shape, texture, and smell. Have your child sort his or her collection according to some characteristic, such as living or nonliving, different colors, rough or smooth, and so on. Teach your child to respect the environment by returning the items to the places where they were found.

Magnify It—Children at this age are fascinated by the use of magnifying glasses. Inexpensive ones can be purchased at a local toy store. Have your child draw a picture of one item from the nature hike. Have him or her draw the item again after looking at it with the magnifier. Discuss what he or she observes.

Animal Life—Animals can be studied in a variety of ways. Take a family trip to a zoo! If your child has a pet, discuss the things the pet needs in order to survive. Check out a book on an animal your child would like to learn more about from the library. Encourage your child to discover these things:

* what the animal's offspring look like

* special names for the male, female, and young (Example: elephant—bull, cow, calf)

* its life cycle

* what it eats

* where it lives

* how it moves

* what sounds it makes and why

* how it protects itself

* what characteristics it has that make it a bird, mammal, reptile, fish, amphibian, insect, or other type of animal

Animals that are no longer living—dinosaurs, mammoths, saber-toothed cats—are incredibly interesting to children. If there is a museum nearby with dinosaur or other fossils, be sure to visit it. If not, books on this topic are easy to find and fun to read.

Earth Science

Rock Hunting—Children like to pick up unusual rocks! Your child can start his or her own rock collection. Buy a few pretty ones for inexpensive souvenirs when you are on vacation. Once your child shows an interest, find a book that shows how to classify rocks. Ask your child to describe each rock's attributes (its color, texture, hardness, size, and shape).

"Weather" You Like It or Not—A good way to get children to observe the weather is to have them look outside before they get dressed, and then dress appropriately. Reading or listening to the weather report is also helpful. Children can be very frightened by high winds, lightning and thunder, heavy rain, hail, and other weather phenomena. By finding out what causes the changes in our weather, their fears may be calmed. Here are some children's books that tell about types of weather:

* *Flash, Crash, Rumble, and Roll* by Franklyn M. Branley (Crowell, 1985)

* *The Magic School Bus Inside a Hurricane* by Joanna Cole (Scholastic, 1995)

MORE SCIENCE ACTIVITIES

Earth Science

Earth's Water—Water is one of Earth's most important resources. It is one reason our planet can support life. Here are some water activities to do with your child:

* Study a globe to compare how much of the Earth is covered by water and how much by land. Which covers more?

* Discuss the kinds of life you may find in fresh water versus salt water.

* Predict whether objects will sink or float in fresh water and in salt water. Then test them. (Be sure to try an egg. It sinks in fresh water and floats in salt water.)

Beyond Our Planet—

Children are fascinated by space even though it is difficult for them to understand the vast sizes and distances within the solar system and the universe. Try some of these activities with your young astronomer:

* Look at the moon each night for a month. Watch and record its changing phases.

* Study the night sky using a telescope, binoculars, or the naked eye. Which constellations can you identify?

* Use chalk to draw a model of the solar system on your sidewalk.

Physical Science

Magnet Discoveries—Magnets are great fun and great learning tools! Gather about a dozen different items from around the house. Ask your child to predict which items will be attracted to the magnet and which will not. Then have your child test each item. Let your child find things in the house that use magnets.

Light and Shadows—Studying shadows is an interesting way to study light. Challenge your child to discover answers to these questions:

* What makes a shadow outdoors?

* What makes a shadow indoors?

* When is your outdoor shadow tall? When is it small?

* How do you make an indoor shadow dark and clear? How do make it light and fuzzy?

Then play Shadow Tag with your child. Instead of tagging the other person's body, try to step on his or her shadow.

When the Lights Go Out!—What would happen if the electricity went out at your home? Discuss how many things in the house use electricity. How could your family be prepared for a blackout? What might happen to cause a blackout in your area?

Social Studies Skills
Second Graders Need

Second-grade social studies consists of the children learning about themselves first, and continues in ever-expanding concentric circles until they are studying their families, neighborhoods, communities, states, countries, and the world, both in the past and in the present.

Children learn about people who make a difference in their own lives and people who made a difference in the past. People who make a difference in a child's world are those who care for them, like you! In addition to parents and other family members, a child's grandparents and family ancestors from long ago have made a difference in his or her life. Children use a globe and a world map to locate where family members came from. They gain a sense of history as they look to the past. We each come from a culture that has special festivals, games, traditions, dress, manners, and customs. Children learn to appreciate and respect individuals from many cultures, now and long ago. They also compare and contrast life here and in other countries.

Children progress from studying about themselves, to studying their families, and then the people in their local neighborhood. They begin to learn about the people who supply our wants and needs, and learn the difference between the two. As they identify things they would like to have (their wants), they enter into discussions about earning, spending, and saving money.

In any neighborhood there are people who supply goods and services that we all need, such as police officers, firefighters, postal workers, grocers, bakers, garbage collectors, and doctors. By focusing on the many people who work in a neighborhood, children learn how dependent we are on each other, and how important it is to work together.

While learning about the neighborhood and community, children explore maps. They learn these concepts:

* There are many kinds of maps and they show different information—street maps, city or county maps, park maps, museum maps, zoo maps, trail maps, product maps, state maps, U.S. maps, world maps, globes, and more.

* Maps use symbols (pictures) to represent things. The legend, or key, explains what the symbols mean.

* A compass rose shows directions. (Second graders learn north, south, east, and west.)

Each time children celebrate a holiday such as Valentine's Day, St. Patrick's Day, or Memorial Day, they learn a little more of our country's customs and traditions. They also learn about extraordinary people who have made a difference in our country's history, like Christopher Columbus, the Pilgrims, George Washington, Abraham Lincoln, and Martin Luther King, Jr. Much of our nation's history is embedded in our holidays.

SOCIAL STUDIES ACTIVITIES

All About Me!

If you filled in a baby book after your child was born, this would be a good time to share that with him or her. Photo albums can also help a child to see his or her own growth and development. Even though your child has only been here for about seven years, a lot has happened already. Point out the many events that have already occurred, such as your child's first tooth, first words, first steps, first day at school, birthday parties, holiday events, and perhaps the birth of another child.

Our Family Tree

Sketch out your family tree, including grandparents on both sides, aunts, uncles, and cousins. If you're really ambitious, add photos to go with it. Some stores have picture frames with a family tree drawn, so all you have to do is add the pictures.

Grandparent Interviews

Let your child interview his or her grandparents using page 92 as a guide. If you have a cassette recorder or camcorder, record your child talking with each grandparent. This will become a special family keepsake, especially as your child grows older and grandparents are no longer living.

Needs and Wants

Children at this age need to learn the difference between a need and a want. Needs are things we must have to live, such as food, shelter, air, water, clothing, and love. Wants are things we would like to have but can live without, such as new toys! Create a list with your child of his or her needs and wants.

Beginning Economics

Many children believe that the way their parents get money is to simply write a check or go to the bank to get it! They need to learn the concept that you earn money by working (supplying goods or services to others).

Your child may already have certain responsibilities at home, such as making the bed, cleaning his or her room, or feeding a pet. If your child does not receive an allowance, you may want to begin giving one, making clear what must be done to receive it. Weekly work charts with stars will help your child see his or her progress.

If your child has a special want, give him or her the opportunity to do extra tasks to earn the money, such as raking leaves, taking out the trash, or helping you with the dishes. Encourage your child to save some money each week to buy a larger ticket item in the near future. Saving for a college education is too far away for children. (But not too far for parents to think about!)

 FS-23003 Skills for Success for Your Second Grader • © Frank Schaffer Publications, Inc.

MORE SOCIAL STUDIES ACTIVITIES

Neighborhood Map

On a large sheet of paper, sketch out a simple map of your local neighborhood with your child, starting with your own house and friend's houses. Ask your child what other places he or she has been to or seen, and draw them in as you talk. Include the school, fire station, police station, library, market, bakery, coffee shop, pet store, or other places of interest. Discuss the need for each of these places, which supply goods (food, baked goods, pet supplies), and which supply services (medical care, postal delivery).

Each time you travel to different parts of the community, point out the different types of businesses and the need for each. Discuss how your neighborhood has changed since you moved there, and why those changes have taken place.

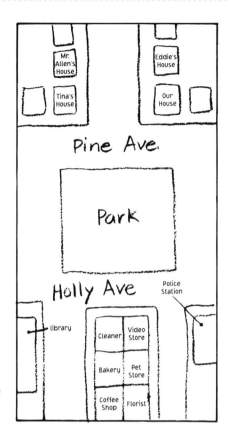

Reading a Map

Use page 93 to help your child learn how to read a map. Show your child any city or state maps you may have and how you use them. (Your phone book may have a map that includes your street.) Graduate to a map of the country, a world map, and a globe, pointing out the similarities and differences they all have.

Go on a Treasure Hunt!

Hide a treasure of some kind—cookies maybe! Write treasure clues on separate pieces of paper, each of which directs your child to the next clue and finally to the treasure. Try about five or six clues in all. If you have a compass, include the directions north, south, east, and west. This is great fun!

> Go straight out the back door until you reach the grass. Turn left and walk six steps. You will find your next clue there.

Holiday Time

Each time a holiday is celebrated, tell your child how you celebrated it as a child yourself. Your own family traditions are being established as you have family get-togethers for Thanksgiving, Hanukkah or Christmas, birthdays, and so on. What will your child remember about Valentine's Day or Halloween costumes when he or she is an adult? These are all extremely exciting to children at this age. As adults, we tend to forget the anticipation and excitement we felt as children when these special events occurred. Literature Tip! Edna Barth's *Turkeys, Pilgrims, and Indian Corn* (Clarion, 1975) is one in her series of books that explains the history of holiday symbols.

Art Skills
Second Graders Need

The classroom teacher or art teacher will provide activities for children to study elements of art such as line, shape, and color. Specific art projects for each of these elements allow children to explore how to creatively combine them. Works of famous artists may be studied to show how they used the featured elements.

Second graders often work with a variety of art materials, such as pencil, pastels, charcoal, magic markers, watercolors, tempera paint, yarn, mosaic pieces, construction paper, papier-mâché, and clay.

Children are introduced to the primary colors (red, yellow, and blue) and learn how to mix them to make the secondary colors (orange, green, and purple).

You will find the use of art woven into other parts of the curriculum. Studying colors and how they are made often leads to a study of rainbows in science. Children may illustrate the beginning, middle, and end to a story they read or wrote. In social studies, second graders sometimes make globes by papier-mâchéing balloons and painting them. Your child might make a mask or costume for a class play.

Art in the primary grades often includes holiday and seasonal projects—pine cone turkeys at Thanksgiving, snowflakes in winter, paper lanterns for Chinese New Year, and bright flowers in spring.

Help your child gain an appreciation of art in his or her life. Visual images that appeal to children surround them. Compare and analyze the styles of illustrators of children's books. Can you recognize books illustrated by Tomie dePaola? How do the borders add to the story in many of Jan Brett's books? Children enjoy cartoons and animated movies. Their favorite characters can be found on backpacks, lunch boxes, shirts, and hats. It would be a dull, colorless world if it were not for the artists of the world, both past and present.

The goal of art in the classroom is not to produce a lot of little Michelangelos, but to give children an opportunity to explore and express themselves in a variety of mediums. When your child brings home a painting, instead of asking "What is it?" say "Tell me about it." You may even want to write down what he or she says. Be sure to date it. Keep one or two of your child's best endeavors each year. These will become treasures in the years to come.

ART ACTIVITIES

Nature Hunt Collage

Any time of year is good for a nature hike, but fall seems to yield the most interesting items. Gather leaves, twigs, or flowers with your child. Make a collage by gluing the items onto a large piece of construction paper or cardboard, an open paper bag, or a plastic foam tray.

Sandpaper Prints

Have your child draw a brightly colored picture on sandpaper. Lay the picture on the ironing board with a piece of plain paper on top of it. Put a press cloth over both and press the iron down firmly. Remove the cloth and admire the imprint on the plain paper. You can re-color the sandpaper and do this again!

Recycle Your Crayons

Put paper cups in a muffin tin. Have your child peel the paper off old crayons. Break the crayons into small pieces, put them in the cups, and bake them at 400° until the crayons just start to melt. (Or microwave them in a non-metal dish.) Don't melt them completely or you will have muddy brown. Let them cool and then remove the paper. Now your child has great multi-colored crayons to use for pictures.

Seed Mosaics

Hunt in the kitchen cupboards to find seeds and grains, such as popcorn kernels, lentils, beans, rice, and macaroni. Arrange them to make a picture and glue them to a plastic foam tray. (White glue dries clear.) If the weather is good, let your child work outside so the birds can snack on the leftovers!

Colorful Cookery

Let your child experiment with the primary colors using frosting, food coloring, and six bowls. Divide some white frosting into three bowls. Add a few drops of red, yellow, or blue food coloring to each bowl for your child to mix with the frosting. Use the other bowls to let your child discover the secondary colors. Use one bowl to mix some yellow and blue frosting (green), one to mix some blue and red frosting (purple), and one to mix some red and yellow frosting (orange).

Make sugar cookies. Let your child be creative and frost them. Use small items for decorations, such as raisins, red hots, or candy corn. You've heard of wearable art—this is edible art!

MORE ART ACTIVITIES

Bead Necklaces

For this project you can use colorful magazine pages or just colored construction paper. Cut long triangular pieces of paper as shown. Starting at the large end, have your child roll the paper on a pencil, gluing the tip at the end. Once your child has made a set of beads, he or she can string them on yarn or string.

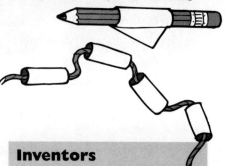

Inventors Extraordinaire!

For one week, collect all usable trash for your child to use to make an invention. Save items such as toilet paper rolls, cereal boxes, plastic bottles, and lids. Set up your child at an indoor or outdoor workspace with glue, scissors, masking tape, string, yarn, brads, or other materials. Challenge your child to create a new invention, with a moving part, if possible. You may be surprised how clever he or she is!

Rub-a-Dub-Dub

Peel the paper off some crayons or use the recycled crayon from page 39. Lay a piece of paper on top of different textured objects. Hold the crayon sideways and rub over the paper. What happens? Inside the house, try coins, a cheese grater, keys, a paper clip, or the sole of a shoe. Outside the house, try tree bark, a leaf, a brick, or the sidewalk. Have a fun day!

Make Your Own Vase

Recycle used bottles and jars with this project. Have your child tear small pieces of masking tape (you may need to do this for your child) and overlap the pieces on a bottle until it is completely covered. Rub brown shoe polish on the tape pieces, using a rag. You will get an interesting effect. Now you are ready to fill it with flowers!

Sidewalk Artists

Look for an inexpensive bucket of sidewalk chalk at a discount department store. Then let your child use the chalk to draw pictures and scenes outside. If you dip the chalk in a bowl of water, it will make a creamier, brighter color. (It will also use up the chalk much quicker.) You may want your child to wear an old T-shirt to keep the chalk off his or her clothes. The drawings will eventually fade or you can wash them off with a hose.

Oldie, But Goodie

On a small piece of white paper, have your child color blocks of bright colors to cover the entire page. Then have your child completely color over the colors with black crayon or black paint. (If you use paint, let it dry before the next step.) Direct your child to use a paper clip or other small scraping device to draw a picture. The colors beneath will be revealed to make a striking picture.

Music Skills
Second Graders Need

Musical experiences for second graders will include listening, singing, moving, and performing to music from their own region and cultural group and to that of others. The world of music is derived from a wide variety of backgrounds!

Children will learn how to listen for different aspects of music. They may be asked to identify high and low sounds, loud and soft sections, or the tempo (speed) of a piece. Second graders can begin to imitate rhythmic patterns by clapping their hands or tapping their fingertips on their thighs, knees, or desk. They may also move to the rhythm by hopping, jumping, trotting, galloping, or skipping. Second graders can even improvise their own creative movements.

A favorite activity for many second graders is creating their own musical accompaniments using classroom instruments such as rhythm sticks, tone bells, sandpaper blocks, castanets, drums, tambourines, or maracas.

Children can participate in singing all kinds of songs that may be integrated into what they are already learning in other subject areas. In this grade in particular, children can use their knowledge of songs to help themselves become better readers. The integration of music with language helps children make important connections. Remember, your child probably learned the ABCs by singing the "Alphabet Song." By singing songs with simple words, he or she can learn to read those words also!

Schoolwide assemblies may include a visit from a district choral or band group, or even a professional one. Sometimes second graders take a field trip to a local theater for a musical production. This is a good time for them to be taught proper audience behavior.

Even though children get nervous in front of an audience, they love to sing and perform songs for their schoolmates or parents. Oftentimes, children will add their own verses to a popular song they have sung in class. Adventurous ones will even add a simple dance routine. Some children are real actors and actresses when it comes to dramatizing songs for special programs.

MUSIC ACTIVITIES

Music Resources

You don't need a musical background to help your child enjoy and appreciate music. Here are several resources to help you out.

Favorite Performers—Your library or local music store should have a children's section with tapes, CDs, or records. Look for recordings by these favorites: Hap Palmer, Raffi, Greg & Steve, Sweet Honey in the Rock, and Peter, Paul, & Mary.

Musical Books—Check local toy or book stores for books that have a sound strip down the right side. As children turn the pages, a visual clue shows them what to press to hear a sound effect or song. These are great fun and you will find your child returning to them time and time again!

Musical Videos—When you go to the video rental store, keep your eyes open for musicals your child may enjoy, such as *The Sound of Music* or *Muppet Treasure Island*, and for music videos, such as the Kids Songs or Disney's Sing-Along series.

Books With Cassettes—Many publishers have put song books together with a cassette tape so children can follow along. (The Wee Sing series is one example.) This is an excellent way for your child to increase his or her vocabulary almost effortlessly. Start a simple colored dot system to keep all of these organized. Put the same color dot on the book, the cassette, and a sealed plastic bag, so your child can put them away neatly.

Picture Books—There are many picture-book versions of popular songs that are fun to sing along with or read. *Jane Yolen's Mother Goose Songbook* by Jane Yolen (Boyd's Mills Press, 1992) gives a brief history of many Mother Goose rhymes as well as the lyrics and musical arrangements.

Look for these titles as well:

Cat Goes Fiddle-i-Fee
Down by the Bay
Lift Ev'ry Voice and Sing
Old MacDonald Had a Farm
The Star-Spangled Banner
Take Me Out to the Ball Game
There Was an Old Lady Who Swallowed a Fly
The Twelve Days of Christmas
This Old Man

A Family Outing

Check local theater groups for their latest musical productions, such as *The Nutcracker, Annie,* or *Oliver.* Find out if your library sponsors a music series for children. Or keep your eyes open for a symphony performance of *Peter and the Wolf.* This makes for a nice family afternoon or evening, and is a great way to encourage music appreciation.

Rainy Day Activity

You can combine art and music on a rainy day. Turn on the radio or stereo and let your child color or paint a picture as he or she listens to songs. This can lead to a great discussion of how music makes you feel and how that can be expressed in art.

Whistle While You Work

While working alongside your child doing the dishes or raking leaves, sing a song you both know. The time will go faster! If you are really adventurous, try singing a round, such as "Row, Row, Row Your Boat" or "Frère Jacques."

MUSICAL INSTRUMENTS

A Musical Gift

For birthday or holiday gifts, consider buying a musical gift or instrument of some kind, such as a xylophone, an electronic keyboard, bells, a recorder or toy flute, or a microphone for sing-alongs. Or make your own with the ideas that follow.

Make Your Own Instruments!

Make **rhythm sticks** from dowels, a half-inch to one-inch thick and 12 inches long. Shellac or paint them. Then have your child use them to tap out the beat to a song.

Your child can rub together two **sandpaper blocks** to get a great shuffling sound. To make them, you'll need two blocks of wood about 4" x 6" and three-quarters of an inch thick. Cover the bottom and side of each block with a sheet of sandpaper, rough side up. Glue or tack it down.

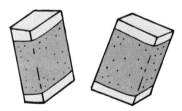

Make a **drum** from a salt container. Your child can tap the top with the rubber end of a pencil. If you leave some salt inside, you can use it as a rattle too!

Turn a **balloon** into a simple sound instrument. Put three or four paper clips into the balloon before blowing it up and tying it off. What kind of sound do you get when you shake it? Find out!

Make another kind of **shaker** by adding beans, pebbles, or marbles to a paper bag, blowing it up, and closing the end with a rubber band. You can also add any of those items to an empty egg carton and tape it closed. Now shake it!

A **tambourine** is easy to make and fun to play. You will need two foil pie pans and some beans. Put the beans in one pan, invert the other pan on top, and staple the edges together.

A Wonderful CD-ROM

If you have a computer with a CD-ROM drive, you may want to purchase Musical Instruments by Microsoft. This software uses images and sound clips to introduce children to a variety of instruments and musical ensembles from around the world.

Physical Education Skills Second Graders Need

In general, we want our children to participate confidently in many different forms of physical activity. We also want them to value physical fitness and understand that both physical activity and physical fitness are important to a person's health and well-being.

As children participate in physical activity, they will develop a variety of motor skills that are related to lifetime leisure activities, as well as gaining the knowledge of rules and strategies of many games and sports. Second graders can have a great deal of fun as they learn new skills and games. Their self-confidence and self-worth will improve, which in turn, will help them in the classroom. Healthy body, healthy mind! See page 94 for a helpful physical skills record sheet.

Children will continue to do physical activities that improve their motor skills, such as walking, running, hopping, jumping, galloping, and skipping. And they will learn to do these without bumping into others or falling!

Second graders work on their eye-hand coordination by focusing on activities such as throwing, catching, hitting, and bouncing balls. To develop eye-foot coordination, children may practice kicking and dribbling a soccer ball. Jumping rope and using a Hula-Hoop are activities that develop a child's overall body coordination.

Body-image skills include being able to name and know where all of your body parts are and to use them as you exercise. Other body-image skills are being able to not touch others when you are moving and to travel in relationship to objects, such as going over, under, behind, and through objects in an obstacle course.

Second graders also work on balance skills and do rhythm activities during their physical education classes.

As children progress to practicing their newly-learned skills in a game, they will be expected to play safely and by the rules, use the equipment properly, and cooperate with their teammates and show them respect. They also need to exhibit good sportsmanship, whether they win or lose.

Your child may be participating in a sport outside of school hours, such as soccer, gymnastics, or basketball. This is an excellent opportunity for you to observe your child's actual skills, as well as his or her ability to display good sportsmanship. Remember that children learn a great deal through example, so be sure you are modeling what you expect from them! This holds true for your own participation in physical activities, too.

Before, during, and after sport-type activities, be sure to discuss with your child what he or she is feeling as a result of the challenges, successes, and failures faced. Positive comments and encouragement will go a long way at these times.

PHYSICAL EDUCATION ACTIVITIES

Move, Move, Move!

Most children don't have any trouble walking or running! In fact, both parents and teachers alike are usually trying to slow them down. However, hopping, particularly on their non-dominant leg, is tricky for many of them. To practice this skill, have your child race you to a certain point, hopping on one foot, then hopping back on the other. Keep the distance short. Try jumping on two feet next. Skipping requires quite a bit of coordination, but practice makes perfect!

Follow the Bouncing Ball

If your child has trouble bouncing a ball, it may be because he or she only "pats" the ball. Encourage your child to "push" it down. Once your child can stand in place and bounce the ball, he or she is ready to move around and dribble it in different directions.

Handball and four-square are two other games that will improve your child's ball-bouncing skills.

Coordinating Eyes and Hands

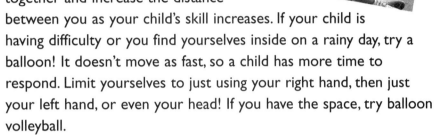

Any kind of ball, especially soft sponge balls, can be used for throwing and catching. Beanbags are good also. Start with the two of you close together and increase the distance between you as your child's skill increases. If your child is having difficulty or you find yourselves inside on a rainy day, try a balloon! It doesn't move as fast, so a child has more time to respond. Limit yourselves to just using your right hand, then just your left hand, or even your head! If you have the space, try balloon volleyball.

Save a couple of plastic milk jugs. Cut out the bottom to make a scoop. You can then toss and catch small balls with them! If you don't have any small balls, roll some newspaper into a small wad and cover it with masking tape.

Bean-Bag Launcher

Build a sturdy launcher or improvise with materials on hand. To build one, start with a piece of sanded wood about 2 feet long, 6 inches wide, and one half inch thick. Take a 6 inch piece of round dowling about 1 inch thick, and shave off one edge slightly so you have a flat surface. Nail the flat surface of the dowel to the larger board as shown. If you wish paint the whole board.

Make or buy several beanbags. Place one beanbag at the far end of the launcher board and stomp on the other end with your foot. The beanbag will launch into the air for your child to catch! When your child gets good at catching a beanbag using both hands, encourage him or her to try the right hand only, then the left. Ready for a challenge? Try two beanbags at a time, then three or more. Everyone in the family will enjoy this activity.

MORE P.E. ACTIVITIES

Mirror Image

Face your child and tell him or her to do exactly what you do with your body. Begin with simple movements such as slowly raising one hand. Build to more complex actions, such as bending your legs while moving both hands in different directions.

Kicking Skills

Set up two objects about 10 feet apart and have your child stand between them about 20 feet away. Have your child kick the ball between the two objects, using the instep of the foot. Decrease the distance between the two objects so your child has to be more accurate with his or her kicks.

Kick the Can

Set up several cans along the ground for your child to kick over. See how many tries it takes to knock them all over.

Ball Control

You can also stack cans in columns two or three cans high for your child to weave in and out as he or she kicks a soccer ball using feet or dribbles a basketball ball using hands.

Jump Rope

Jumping rope is not an easy skill since it involves overall body coordination. If your child has difficulty, put the rope on the ground and have him or her jump on the left side, then on the right, to get the jumping motion first. Then move to having your child jump over a rope as it is swung back and forth like a pendulum. Once your child can do this, begin to turn the rope over his or her head. When your child masters this skill, he or she is ready for a small individual rope.

Have your child practice jumping forward in place, until that skill is mastered. Then your child can try jumping backwards. If you want to burn some calories, get a jump rope for yourself, too!

Balance Skills

To practice balance skills, you can draw a chalk line on a sidewalk or use a long two-by-four board. Ask your child to try these skills:

* walk forward

* walk forward with a beanbag on your head

* walk backward, with and without a beanbag

* slide sideward

* walk sideward, crossing one foot over and in front of the other

* balance on one foot and then the other

* balance with eyes open and then closed

* stand on one foot and swing the other leg back and forth with eyes open, and then with eyes closed

Social Skills Second Graders Need

TEAMS AND CLUBS

If your child is to succeed at school and in life, he or she will need social skills in addition to academics. This section of the book focuses on activities that promote those skills.

Every child is a unique individual, with his or her own special abilities and interests. In addition to a child's family responsibilities and schoolwork, a child's outside interests can add a great deal to the development of his or her social skills. Encourage your child to join in activities, but do not push. Remember the key is balance.

Sports

A variety of team sports are available to youngsters at this age, such as soccer, baseball, and basketball. Gymnastics, dance, and karate lessons are also popular. All of these will help your child develop responsibility, self-discipline, physical skills, teamwork, and self-confidence.

If you have a local YMCA, check to see what children's programs it has. Many have a pool and offer swimming and diving lessons during the summer and throughout the schoolyear.

Clubs

Your child may have the opportunity to join Cub Scouts, Brownies, or Camp Fire Girls. These groups provide a variety of outdoor and indoor activities that children enjoy. In some communities, 4-H clubs are popular. The four H's are head, heart, hands, and health. If your child has a special interest in plants and animals, this is an organization that may appeal to him or her.

Some groups pair up dads with their daughters or moms with their sons to give parents opportunities to spend time with both their sons and their daughters.

Does your child like to act or sing? Many local theater groups support young fledging actors, actresses, and singers!

Your child may want to play the piano, collect stamps, or be part of a computer group. Whatever special interest your child has, there is probably a group where he or she can share that interest.

Remember, your child may not have the same interests as you. Allow your child to develop his or her individuality. Everyone is good at something. Help your child find the activity in which he or she can shine. Give your child all the support he or she needs!

Be sure not to overload your child. One or two extra-curricular activities is fine. But if your child has soccer practice, music lessons, art class, science club, and scouts each week, he or she won't have time to be a kid. Children need off-time so they can relax and play.

GETTING ALONG WITH SIBLINGS

One of the most difficult things parents have to deal with when they have more than one child is teaching those children how to get along with each other. Children need to learn how to resolve their own conflicts as much as possible. How to deal with siblings is a skill children can then apply to dealing with classmates and friends.

Children's constant tattling on each other can strain any parent's patience! Teach your children the difference between tattling and reporting. *Tattling* is when you're trying to get someone in trouble. *Reporting* is when someone needs help.

Discuss the situations below with your children. Tell them to decide if each one is a situation that would cause tattling or reporting.

When one of your children comes to tell you something that another child is doing, ask "Why are you telling me?" The answer to that question will reveal whether they are tattling or reporting.

If the child is tattling, ask him or her what a more appropriate action would be. Teach your child to deal with the situation by telling the other child the following:

I don't like it when you _____.
or

I want you to _____.

Here are two sample conversations:

Child: Mom, Jason fell and cut his knee!

Mom: Where is he?

Child: In the backyard on the patio.

(After the mother takes care of Jason, she thanks the child for *reporting*—for letting her know Jason needed help.)

Child: Dad, Cathy keeps taking my basketball!

Dad: Why are you telling me?

Child: Because I want her to stop!

Dad: Then you need to say, "I don't like it when_____."

Child: OK, OK, I know.

Child: Cathy, I don't like it when you take my ball away from me. I want you to leave it alone.

Cathy: Well, I don't like it when you won't let me play with you.

Child: OK—How about you let me shoot a basket, then I'll let you shoot a basket? We'll take turns.

Cathy: Deal!

Eventually, you will begin to hear your children settle their own conflicts, without you having to be the referee every time.

* **Your sister takes a book away from you.**

* **Your brother eats your last cookie.**

* **Your baby brother falls and is crying.**

* **Your sister won't give you back your doll.**

* **Your sister cuts her finger.**

* **Your brother pushes you out of a chair.**

* **Your brother bangs his head on the cement wall outside.**

* **Your sister won't give you a turn on the swing.**

HOME RESPONSIBILITIES

There are several other areas of responsibility that need to be addressed by the time a child is in second grade. Remember the adage, "Never do anything a child can do." As parents, we have a tendency to do too much for our children, which does not allow them to grow in their capabilities and independence.

Getting Ready in the Morning

In the morning, your child should be responsible enough to get dressed, help a little with breakfast and lunch preparation, brush his or her teeth, and gather belongings to take to school (such as backpack with homework, jacket, lunch, sharing item). Of those things listed above, what can your child do already? What step could he or she take next?

In addition, you may require your child to make his or her bed and clean up the bedroom and bathroom. Can your child straighten up his or her toys, put books on a shelf, hang up clothes, put dirty clothes in a hamper? If not, why not? Are you doing the job for your child? Add to your child's responsibilities, not to yours!

Chores

Here are some other daily tasks children may be able to do at this age:

* set the table
* help prepare dinner
* clear and wipe off the table
* rinse and load his or her own dishes into the dishwasher
* put away clean silverware
* feed a pet and put out fresh water for it
* clean a pet's cage
* start homework without being told

Weekly chores your second grader may be able to do include these:

* fold and put away his or her laundry
* dust
* pick up and bag newspapers for recycling
* gather and empty all the trash cans around the home
* clean the bathroom counters and sinks
* sweep or vacuum his or her own bedroom

And don't forget outdoor chores:

* rake leaves
* pick up litter
* water the flowers or lawn
* pull weeds

The idea is not to overwhelm a child with work, but to give him or her opportunities to grow and mature. If you set a regular chore time when the entire family is busy working, it makes everyone feel they are doing their part and not being singled out.

MORE HOME RESPONSIBILITIES

Getting Ready in the Evening

At bedtime, your child's responsibilities might be to get dressed for bed, brush his or her teeth, choose clothes for the next day, and get his or her backpack ready, including homework. THEN you can read a bedtime story!

Rewards

Be sure to give praise to your child for tasks he or she accomplishes. A chart that lists daily responsibilities can be put on the refrigerator, with stars added when each task is completed. If desired, offer a small reward for a good week, such as a yogurt or ice-cream cone, rental of a special movie, staying up an hour later on Friday, or a sleepover of a special friend.

The eventual goal is for your child to contribute because that is what is needed and expected of each family member. Some people object to rewards for doing what needs to be done. Do what works best for your family.

Home Responsibility Tips

Most children just need a reminder or redirection with their responsibilities. If your child says he or she is ready for school or ready for bed, ask "What have you done so far? What do you still have to do? Oh good, you remembered!"

One helpful technique for getting kids to work is to make a game out it. See if your child can beat a timer. You can use a five-minute egg timer or the wind up kind, or set the delay timer on the microwave. Ask your child how long he or she thinks the task will take. This idea can really motivate children to move! Another motivator is to have your child race you. Give your child a friendly challenge, such as this: Can you finish cleaning your room before Dad finishes giving the baby a bath and I finish the dishes?

If after a reminder or redirection your child still does not complete a task, there needs to be a consequence. Appropriate consequences might be one of these:

* no friends over to play
* no T.V.
* no computer play
* no star on the chart
* time alone in the bedroom to think
* an earlier bedtime

One thing is certain. The more responsibility your child develops at home, the more responsible he or she will be at school and throughout life. And that will spell SUCCESS!

FOLLOWING RULES

Every household has its own rules and every classroom and school has its rules as well. All through life your child will be expected to follow rules—at home, at school, at work, in society.

Family Discussion

A good discussion to have in your family is why rules are needed at all. Ask your child questions such as these:

✸ What if no one stopped at red lights?

✸ What if people drove as fast as they wanted to?

✸ What if people took whatever they wanted from others?

Let that discussion lead to rules at home.

✸ What would happen if everyone in the family left his or her belongings everywhere in the house?

✸ What if you left out every game you played with?

✸ What would happen if you always left your bike in the driveway?

Household Rules

Household rules need to be fair, clearly explained, and applied equally to all children. Remember to be firm, consistent, and loving.

When your child follows a rule, be generous in your praise.

Children need to know that you "say what you mean, and mean what you say." If a rule is not followed, there needs to be a consequence. For instance, if your child does not put away a game, that game could be put away in the garage for a week. If your child is watching T.V. before homework is done, then the T.V. goes off, the homework gets done, and the T.V. does not go back on for the rest of the evening, or the child goes to bed earlier.

Other consequences for your child could be a "time out" in his or her room.

School Rules

Be sure to support school and classroom rules. If the teacher has indicated there is a behavior problem with your child, be sure to follow up. Work with the teacher so your child knows that your expectations and the teacher's coincide. Your child cannot succeed in school without following the rules. If your personal beliefs differ strongly with a school rule, meet privately with your child's teacher. Most times an alternative can be agreed to that respects the needs and wishes of both parties.

Love Your Child!
Never withdraw your love from your child when he or she misbehaves. Make it clear that it is the behavior you do not like, not him or her. As soon as your child does turn around negative behavior, be sure to praise him or her for it. The more positive you are overall, the less problems you will have with your child misbehaving. Try it!

PROBLEM SOLVING

1. **What is the problem?**
2. **What are the fair ways it could be solved?**
3. **What are the advantages and disadvantages of each solution?**
4. **Which one will you choose?**

Problem-Solving Process

Like adults, children run into problems that need to be solved everyday. Their problems may be different than adults', but the problem-solving process is still the same.

The entire process does not need to be used for every problem, but if your child learns to think about solving little problems, the process will be internalized for the bigger ones.

Classroom Examples

Here are two scenarios that show how a teacher might direct a child's thinking in class:

Child: I can't find my pencil.

Teacher: How can you solve that problem?

Child: I could get one out of the pencil can.

Teacher: You're right. What if the pencil can is empty?

Child: I could borrow one from a friend.

Teacher: You're a good thinker.

Child: I didn't finish my math paper.

Teacher: Why is that?

Child: Ashley kept talking to me.

Teacher: How are you going to solve that problem?

Child: I could tell her to stop.

Teacher: Well, that's one solution. What if that doesn't work?

Child: Maybe I could sit at the extra table.

Teacher: That would probably work, too.

Child: Or I could tell her we need to work together to get our math done before recess.

Teacher: That's another good solution. I'll watch to see which one you choose.

Notice in both examples that the teacher does not tell the children what to do, but encourages them to think about the problem. That way, the children will begin to solve problems on their own.

Role Play

Try this process with your own child. Ask your child what he or she would do in each of these instances:

✳ You forget your lunch.

✳ You don't feel well in class.

✳ You forget it's your sharing day.

✳ You can't open your snack package.

✳ You miss the bus.

Communicate

At the end of the day, ask your child what problems he or she solved that day. Reinforce his or her ability to solve problems. Share what problems you solved, too!

MORE PROBLEM SOLVING

Bigger Problems to Solve

In this day and age, your child needs to be prepared to handle some other situations as well. Sometimes, the only practice you can give your child is playing "What If?"

What if no one is home and the door is locked when you get home from school?

Elicit some alternatives from your child. Is there a hide-away key? Is there a neighbor he or she can go to? Could your child go in the backyard and enter the home some other way? What else?

What if a stranger offers you a ride home from school, even enticing you with candy?

Children are often taught at school to say no, get away, and tell someone. You can reinforce the same procedure without scaring your child. Tell your child you just want him or her to be prepared.

What if the stranger says she knows your mom and dad and they asked her to pick you up?

If the child does not know the person, he or she should not go with them. Tell your child that you would only send a friend or family member the child knows, even in an emergency.

What if another child picks on you?

Teach your child these sentences:

* I don't like it when you (bother me).

* I want you to (leave me alone).

These simple steps will help with brothers and sisters, as well as friends. They will also eliminate you as the middleman. Teach your child to first try to solve his or her problems, without violence. Sometimes, however, we need to step in and speak to another child or his or her parent, or talk to the teacher at school if the problem is occurring there.

What if you are somewhere with the family and you get lost?

Children should always know that a police officer, guard, or other worker in a store or at an event can help

them. If you are going shopping, to a theme park, or another place, establish a policy that if your children lose sight of you, they are to stay put wherever they are. You can be the ones to retrace your steps and find them. It's easier to find each other if only the parents are moving, not the parents and the children!

What if a parent has an accident at home and needs help?

Does your child know how to dial 911? Many children have helped save their parents because they knew what to do in an emergency. Does your child know the house address to give to emergency

personnel? Have your child practice this procedure by holding down the phone button as he or she speaks.

There is no way you can teach your child how to handle every emergency. However, you can teach your child how to think when it comes to solving problems so he or she can handle many situations.

SAFETY

Fire Safety

Children will learn some fire safety at school. They are told not to play with matches and to give any matches they find to an adult. Sometimes a visit from a firefighter or a video will show them what to do if their clothes catch on fire—stop, drop, and roll. Ask your child to demonstrate how to do it. Go over any safety information the teacher sends home.

Fire drills are practiced throughout the year at school so students know how to exit the building and where to assemble outside. Your child needs to know several ways for exiting your home. In addition, the family needs to have an established meeting place outside.

If your child smells smoke and is in a room with a closed door, he or she should feel the door and not open it if it is hot. If you live in a multistory building, talk about how your child could get out through a window and down to the ground.

Traffic Safety

Teach your child how to look both ways before crossing a street, how to cross at a sidewalk, and how to catch a driver's eye to make sure he or she sees you. In a parking lot, point out how cars have white rear lights that go on when the car is moving in reverse. Explain that a driver who is backing up may not see or remember to look for pedestrians.

Bike Safety

If your child has a bike, be sure he or she knows the safety rules for using one. Do you require your child to wear a helmet? Does the law? What are the house rules for how far your child may go on the bike? Does your child have a lock for the bike? Check your community's bike guidelines to see if riders should ride with traffic or facing it. Watch your child to be sure he or she knows how to use hand signals and walks the bike across a crosswalk.

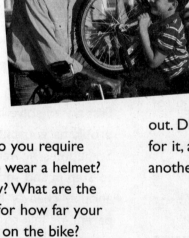

Your child's bike needs to be kept in good repair. It also needs a place to call home, which is not in the driveway where someone may run over it!

Water Safety

Your child may have already had a few years of swimming lessons, but whether you are at a lake, at the beach, or by a swimming pool, be sure your child knows and follows good water safety rules. Children often do not think ahead and may not see the water hazards that you do. Have a discussion before your child goes in the water. If your child chooses not to follow a rule you have established, give him or her a ten-minute time out. Discuss the rule, the need for it, and give him or her another chance, but only one.

FRIENDS

Developing Friendships

Friends are an important part of everyone's life. Have a discussion with your child about friends he or she has now, either in the neighborhood, in sports, or at school. Elicit the types of things friends do that make you want to be friends with them. Talk about your own friends and what you like about them as well.

Ask your child how he or she measures up as a friend. Does your child exhibit the same types of behavior he or she wants in a friend? How could your child be a better friend?

Getting Along With Friends

One problem friends may have is deciding what to do, particularly when one friend wants to do one thing, and the other wants to do something else. Teach your child how to compromise. Perhaps one person could choose an activity first, then the other gets to choose.

Taking Turns

Who goes first, in choosing or in taking turns in a game, can create problems. Teach your child how to play the game "Rock, Scissors, Paper."

Each child starts with a closed fist. On the count of three, each person puts out the hand signal for rock, scissors, or paper:

✳ Rock is indicated with a closed fist.

✳ Scissors is indicated with the index and middle fingers held out like scissors.

✳ Paper is indicated with a flat hand.

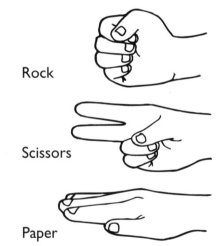

Rock

Scissors

Paper

Each hand signal can win or lose. Rock wins over scissors because it can crush them. Scissors win over paper because they can cut it. Paper wins over rock because it can cover it.

The winner gets to go first. Kids learn this fast and love it!

> Your child's social development is extremely important. The ability to make and foster friendships is an important indicator of how your child's social skills are developing.

Clean Up

Make it a house rule that whatever is taken out or whatever mess is created, it must be cleaned up. Notify the children five minutes before clean-up time. You'll have less trouble bringing the playtime to a close this way.

Problems

Even friends have times when they don't get along. Teach the children the method from the problem-solving page: *I don't like it when you _____. I want you to_____.* If both children have a complaint, let them make a deal. (*How about you_____, and I'll _____.*)

MANNERS

Please, Thank You, You're Welcome

When your child wants something, teach him or her to say "Dad, may I please have_____?" Once the request has been filled, your child says "Thank you" and you say "You're welcome." Reverse roles and ask your child for something so he or she can practice both parts.

The Dinner Table

There are many courtesies a second grader should learn:

* Unless the host says otherwise, don't begin eating until everyone has been seated.

* Place your napkin on your lap.

* Chew with your mouth closed.

* Do not talk with your mouth full.

* Keep your elbows off the table.

* Ask to be excused when you are finished.

Company's Coming!

When guests (adults or children) come to your home, your child can learn to answer the door with a warm greeting, ask them to come in, offer to take their coats, show them into the living room (playroom or bedroom for kids), invite them to sit down, and even ask, "May I get you something to drink?" Your guests will be quite impressed with your child's good manners!

Introductions

Teach your child how to introduce people, always saying the older person's name first:

* Mom, I'd like you to meet my friend Tony.

* Mr. and Mrs. Johnson, this is my younger sister, Janice.

nothing seems to indicate a good upbringing as much as a person's manners. These need to be taught and reinforced at home. Every household is a little different, but as parents, it is your responsibility to teach your child the manners you wish him or her to have.

Interrupting Conversations Politely

One of the most difficult concepts to teach a child is not to interrupt two people when they are talking. Teach your child to wait patiently and then say, "Excuse me, Mom, but there's someone at the door for you." If you are on the phone, teach your child not to interrupt unless it is an emergency.

I'm sorry, that was an accident.

Excuse Me, I'm Sorry

When your child does something accidentally, teach him or her to say "Excuse me" or "I'm sorry." Accidents happen, but rude behavior shouldn't!

CHARACTER DEVELOPMENT

As a parent, you are your child's first teacher. You are the role model your child uses to shape behavior, attitudes, and values. Without your strong guidance, your child may turn to poor role models and give in to the pressures of the peer group.

Strong character does not happen by chance. You will need to help your child develop the types of values, attitudes, and behavior needed to become successful in the classroom, on the job, and in life. Some of these "life skills" are motivation, confidence, hard work, initiative, perseverance, honesty, respect, responsibility, good judgment, problem solving, teamwork, and compassion.

Reading aloud literature that features examples of these life skills is one way to teach them to your child. *The Children's Book of Virtues*, compiled by former Secretary of Education William Bennett (Simon & Schuster, 1995) is an excellent resource. Another collection of stories you might want to look for is *Teach Your Children Well* by Christine Allison (Delacorte, 1993).

In addition, try some of the following activities with your children.

Motivation

"I want to do it!"

A positive attitude is essential in life. "I want to learn more about that" or "I want to be better at this" leads to excitement about learning. Children need to understand that it takes some discipline to stay motivated when you are discouraged. It is helpful to break large tasks into smaller ones, to set and keep time limits, and to give yourself a pat on the back when you do something well.

Share with your child something you were motivated to learn, and how you handled it when you got discouraged. Ask your child what he or she would be interested in learning, such as riding a two-wheel bike, and how he or she could go about it.

Confidence

"I can do it!"

Learning something new, like riding a bike, also helps a child build his or her confidence and an "I can do

it!" attitude. Children at this age have a variety of fears, such as a fear of the dark, fear of lightning and thunder, and so on. They can develop a sense of confidence by carefully looking at their fears and overcoming them one by one.

Discuss with your child what kinds of things he or she is afraid of and why. Ask your child to choose something he or she could become less afraid of and how he or she could make that happen. For instance, if your child is afraid of the dark, consider a night light or a flashlight.

CHARACTER DEVELOPMENT

Being a Hard Worker

"I will work hard!"

If you put in hard work on things you do in life, you will get great results. Being a hard worker means you give your best effort. You will feel even more satisfied when you have done your best on something that was not easy for you.

Discuss with your child some things he or she can do that are easy, things that take a little bit of effort, and things that are hard to do. How does your child approach the more difficult things? Discuss the feelings your child has when he or she accomplishes something that took a lot of hard work. We can all take pride in achievements that come from hard work.

Honesty

"I will tell the truth!"

An honest person tells the truth, even if it means paying for the consequences of one's acts. If people know you are honest, they can trust you and believe what you tell them. All of us are confronted with opportunities where we could lie, cheat, or steal. What we do in those situations determines what kind of person we are.

Both you and your child can share stories of when you have been tempted to be dishonest, what you decided to do, and how you felt about what you did. Be sure to point out the price you have to pay for being dishonest. (People won't believe you even when you tell the truth.)

Good Judgment

"I will use my head!"

Using good judgment often means using common sense, but this sense is not one with which we are born! You need to think before you act and ask yourself "What will happen if I do this?" If you think first, you will probably make better choices. Try to see the other person's point of view before you act. Think about how they feel, and how you would feel in the same situation.

Ask your child what he or she would do in situations such as these:

* It looks like it may rain at school today.

* You have muddy shoes when you get home.

* The water was left running in the kitchen.

* Your baby brother fell down and is crying.

* Your sister dropped all of her crayons on the floor.

Cooperation

"I will work with others!"

A family is a team. Your child needs to learn how to be a member of that home team since this is a skill he or she will need at school, in sports, and on the job. You will need to model and reinforce cooperative behavior.

Choose something that the entire family could do, such as cleaning up the living room, raking leaves, or making dinner. Points out how this builds a sense of togetherness. A large task can be completed more easily if everyone pitches in. "Many hands make light work!" Good cooperation skills will make your child a valuable member of any team.

CHARACTER DEVELOPMENT

Respect and Compassion

"I care about others!"

To show respect for others, you need to let them know you care how they feel. Everyone deserves consideration and needs affection. Simply using thoughtful words can make a difference.

Use little self-sticking notes this week for each member of the family to write something nice to the other family members. "I think you are great because _____."

Your child should also learn to show compassion for those who are less fortunate. Could your family take outgrown clothes to a homeless shelter, donate food to a food bank, give away some toys or books that are in good shape, or contribute to your favorite charity?

Responsibility

"I will do what is right!"

If you are responsible, people can count on you. You *will* do what you say you will, and you *will not do* what you say you will not. Responsible people know what the right thing to do is in any given situation, and they do it. People have a responsibility to themselves, their families, their friends, their schools, their communities, and their planet. Responsible people are in charge of their own behavior.

Discuss the responsibilities each adult in the family has, as well as those each child has. Post a chart that lists your child's responsibilities. Let your child check off each item as he or she does it. Praise your child for being responsible.

Initiative

"I will take some action!"

Initiative involves recognizing something that needs to be done, coming up with an idea, and taking some action to accomplish it. A positive attitude is needed. Even a large goal can be broken into many small steps. "The longest journey begins with the first step."

Children need to learn how to organize things, such as their toy shelves. Besides straightening up their rooms, they practice sorting and classifying—box games, stuffed animals, sports equipment, and so on. Your child could also clean the tool box, straighten a kitchen shelf, or organize his or her closet and dresser.

Perserverance

"I will finish what I start!"

Once you start a job, you need to stick with it until it is done. This may require patience when you start to get discouraged and frustrated. "When the going gets tough, the tough get going." Teach your child not to give up! "If at first you don't succeed, try, try again!" Share some of your own experiences with your child when he or she needs encouragement.

Your child needs perseverance not only when doing homework or cleaning his or her bedroom, but also when learning a new sports skill, such as riding a bike, swimming, or jumping rope.

Home and School Cooperation

GETTING YOUR CHILD ORGANIZED

Have your child pick out the clothes he or she is going to wear the next day and lay them out. This will help you avoid the the last minute rush to find the missing shoe! A sweater or coat can always be added if it is cold. Listen to or read the morning's weather report. To avoid arguments over whether a jacket needs to be worn or not, put a large thermometer outside and decide on a given temperature for jackets. For example, 60° or above, no jacket, 59° or below, on it goes!

By the way, put your child's name on the inside of all jackets, sweaters, and coats!

Your child needs to put homework and any notes that need to go back to school in his or her folder or backpack the night before also. Does your child have a sharing day? If so, the sharing item needs to go in, too. The backpack should always be kept in one spot by the front door so it can be found easily.

Whenever possible, make lunch decisions the night before. If your child is buying

lunch, then lunch money needs to go in the backpack also. If your child is going to take his or her lunch, perhaps he or she can help to make it. Some classes have a snack time. Nutritious snacks like fruit, vegetables, cheese, and crackers will give your child more sustained energy than sugary snacks. Many schools don't allow candy at school at all. Be aware of school rules.

Breakfast time! Can your child help? Remember, never do anything a child can do. Let your child make toast, set the table, pour out the dry cereal, and so on. If pouring milk is too difficult, then you can continue to do it. Encourage your child to become more and more

The key to avoiding harried mornings is to do as much as possible the night before!

independent.

Are there dawdlers in your house? Try this. Time how long it takes your child to get ready, from the time the alarm goes off until he or she goes out the door. If it takes your child one hour and he or she has to leave at 8:00 a.m., then the alarm goes off at 7:00 a.m. If it takes one and a half hours, the alarm goes off at 6:30 a.m. If that's too early for your child to get up, there is an easy solution—bedtime is backed up from 8:30 p.m. to 8:00 p.m. Still too hard to get up? Then bedtime is 7:30 p.m.! This technique will work wonders.

HOMEWORK

Homework is your child's responsibility. Generally, the work itself is not hard, but getting it home, completing it, and getting it back to school on time is the real task! Some teachers hand out a homework assignment each night, Monday through Thursday, while others will give out the week's assignments on Monday to be turned in by Friday.

Amount

Your child's teacher, school, or school district may have a homework policy. It will vary by grade level. Second graders are often required to do about 15 to 30 minutes a day, but the amount of time needed to complete an assignment will vary with each child. If your child does not have assigned homework, you can do any of the activities in this book to supplement schoolwork.

Time and Place

With your child's input, decide which time of day is best for doing homework. It could be right after school or after dinner. The time may need to be flexible if your child has lessons and activities, but stick to the schedule as much as possible. You may want a house rule restricting TV or computer use until homework is done.

A study place should be quiet, have adequate light and workspace, and be equipped with the necessary work tools. Have your child store these items in a desk drawer or homework box so they are easily accessible:

* pencils (several sharpened)
* erasers
* crayons or markers
* paper
* scissors
* glue
* children's dictionary
* calculator (optional—for checking work)

Getting It Done

Offer help and encouragement to your child, but do not do the work for him or her. Help your child read the directions for the assignment, and work through the first problem or two to be sure he or she understands what to do.

If your child has difficulty staying on task, set a goal for the amount of work to be done in the next 10 minutes. You may want to set a timer and challenge your child to see how many problems he or she can do before it buzzes.

If the homework is too difficult or your child consistently feels overwhelmed, speak with your child's teacher. Most will be happy to adapt the homework to fit your child's needs.

Once the work has been completed and you have looked it over, it is your child's responsibility to put it in a folder or backpack right then so it will be ready in the morning. Teachers should never hear, "My dad forgot to put my homework in my backpack."

Praise

Be liberal with your encouragement and praise when your child is putting forth a good effort.

Homework will be one of your best clues as to what your child is learning at school. Remember, your child's work habits are being established now. By showing interest in what your child is doing, he or she will realize how important the schoolwork is.

VOLUNTEERING

Get Involved!

Show your interest in school by being actively involved. With more two-parent working families and single-parent households, schools find it increasingly difficult to get parent help. Don't wait for someone else to do it all. Volunteer! This also shows your child how much you value education and the school.

Be sure to join the school's PTA (Parent Teacher Association). Consider volunteering to be on an advisory committee if you want to be involved in some of the decision-making at school.

If you are available during the day, you could assist with vision and hearing screenings, help on picture day, or organize fundraisers, such as jog-a-thons, carnivals, or school shirts. Your culinary talents will be much appreciated for events like teacher luncheons or bake sales.

Working in your child's classroom is something he or she will enjoy, as well as the rest of the children, and especially the teacher! You can correct papers, run papers on the copy machine, prepare materials for art projects, listen to children read, tend to small scrapes and bumps, file classwork—you name it! You will find it fascinating to see what daily life is really like in your child's classroom, what the teacher and the program are like, and how your child is performing and interacting. You will also gain a new appreciation for teachers and the job they do!

Every classroom can use a Room Parent and that parent can use some help. You may be asked to call on other parents to furnish treats for class parties. Some creative parents will make a simple craft for each child. Make it easy on the teacher by contacting him or her a week or two before a holiday to see what you can do. If you have suggestions, all the better!

Working Parents

If you are a working parent or have a little one, volunteer to help at home. You could correct papers, make games, sew beanbags, collate math packets, translate forms, send treats or punch for a party, donate items for a rummage sale, or make simple costumes for a play.

If you are available during the evening, you could help out with spaghetti dinner fundraisers, Adopt-a-Book Night, parent education events, ice-cream socials, or coffee and cookies for Back-to-School Night.

Do you have a special talent or hobby that could be shared with the class? Could you get a morning off of work to go on a field trip with your child? Do you have a carpentry talent to help with some shelving for books, or hooks for jackets? Everyone can do something!

Time Commitment

Volunteering does not have to be a two-hour a week commitment. Whatever time you can contribute throughout the year will be appreciated by your child and your child's teacher. Remember, the most important work you do is to provide a safe and loving environment at home so your child is ready to learn at school.

SCHOOL EVENTS

Back-to-School Night

One of the first opportunities you will have to visit your child's classroom will be Back-to-School Night, which is usually within the first month of school. This is generally a parent-information night, not an evening for children to attend. Some PTA's provide child care, but if not, do make arrangements for a babysitter.

Some evenings start with a PTA meeting in which the entire staff is introduced. Classroom visitations may be broken into two or more sessions to allow you to visit each room if you have more than one child attending the school. If the evening is not divided into sessions, you may want to have your spouse or other family member attend one of the classroom presentations. If you cannot get to the main presentation at the second (or third) child's room, at least try to stop by briefly to obtain any handouts and to say hello to the teacher.

While agendas will vary, these items are usually covered:

✳ your child's daily schedule

✳ the general content for each subject taught and the materials used

✳ homework routines

✳ what to do if your child is absent

✳ discipline procedures for the school and class

✳ dates for conferences and report cards

More than anything else, you will meet your child's teacher and get a feel for what he or she is like. Your child spends about six hours a day, five days a week, with this adult. Get to know him or her!

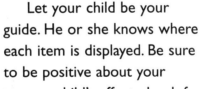

note! This is not conference night. Refrain from asking how your child is doing. The teacher has only had a few weeks to get to know your child and needs to speak momentarily with each parent. Also confidentiality cannot be maintained in a large group.

Open House Night

At Back-to-School Night you find out what your child is going to do, while at Open House you find out what your child has done. This is a major school event and is extremely important to your child, so make every effort to attend. In addition to a PTA meeting to open the evening, many schools offer a social of some kind, before or after the event.

Let your child be your guide. He or she knows where each item is displayed. Be sure to be positive about your child's efforts. Look for samples of your child's reading books, daily work, writing, math work, art and science projects, social studies activities, computer center, and so on. Introduce yourself to the teacher again and make a positive comment about the room to him or her also. This event takes a lot of work! Only take home items if the teacher says it is OK. Many schools have the children "snake through" the other classrooms the next morning to see their work.

There may be other places your child needs to take you besides the classroom such as the library, music room, art room, gym, computer lab, resource or speech room if your child receives those services, the office, or cafeteria. Plan to make an evening of it. Go out for yogurt or ice cream afterwards.

REPORT CARDS AND CONFERENCES

Report Cards

Many schools give report cards on a quarterly basis. Others give report cards three times a year. Find out what is standard at your school so you will know what to expect.

The report card will give you an indication of how well your child is doing in each subject area, as well as in areas of citizenship, work habits, and behavior. Schools vary in their styles of report cards. Some give letter grades and percentages for academic areas. Others give you an idea of where your child is on a continuum of levels in regards to reading, writing, and spelling, and then give grades based on the effort of the child. Still others give a written evaluation for different subjects in place of grades.

Read through the report card with your child. Get his or her input on strengths and weaknesses, and what can be done to improve the latter.

Conferences

Conferences are often scheduled at the end of the first and third quarters. If your school is on a trimester schedule, conferences will probably be at the end of the first and second trimesters.

A conference is invaluable because of the information you and the teacher can give each other. Samples of your child's work, diagnostic tests, and the teacher's daily observations will give you insight as to how your child is doing. Listen for areas that may need improvement and ask for suggestions as to what you can do at home to help. You can help the teacher understand your child better by filling him or her in on family happenings that could be affecting work or behavior, such as the birth of a sibling or a death or serious illness in the family.

Some teachers request the child's presence at a conference, more often at the second conference than the first. In any case, go over the information you have received with your child, focusing on the growth and effort made, as well as areas that need to be improved. Work out a plan for the latter with your child, such as an extra ten minutes of reading each night, going over

math facts, or practicing letter formation. Your interest in your child's education is what makes the critical difference in whether he or she succeeds or not. Work with the teacher to help your child.

If you feel a need to speak with the teacher outside of regularly-scheduled conferences, don't hesitate to send him or her a note requesting that you meet. You can also call the school to ask for a convenient time to see the teacher. Be careful not to interrupt a class that is in session since that is not fair to the rest of the children.

If you see the teacher before or after class, ask when it would be a good time to discuss a concern you have. If the teacher has time right then, he or she will say so. Just be aware that teachers are usually doing last minute preparations before class, and have paper correcting, meetings to attend, and the next day's lessons to prepare after school.

HOME AND SCHOOL COMMUNICATION

From School to Home

Your child will be bringing home tons of material from school! A backpack will help him or her carry it all. An additional folder inside can help your child keep the papers in good shape. Teach your child how to sort through it all.

Homework—Homework that needs to be completed should go in a special place so it doesn't get lost, scribbled on by baby brother, or eaten by the dog!

Corrected Work—This work will give you important clues as to what your child is learning in school and how he or she is doing. When you have a few moments, go over the work with your child, complimenting him or her on work well done and reviewing material that has been missed. Let your child choose his or her best paper to put on the refrigerator for display.

Some papers can be kept in a special folder temporarily. By dating your child's work, you will be able to see the growth he or she is making. You can't keep everything; so

at the end of the year, you and your child can select a few samples of his or her best work as keepsakes and store them in file folders.

Newsletters and Notices—Newsletters can be put aside for reading and discussing together when you have time. Both classroom and school newsletters will let you know what is going on at school. Stay informed. You will also find notices for parents— field trip information, picture day envelopes, conference forms, fundraiser notices, parent helper notes, PTA requests, surveys, flyers for your child to sign up for sports and clubs— you name it, you'll get it! Whatever needs to go back to school should be put in the backpack or folder by your child. This develops his or her responsibility.

From Home to School

The teacher will appreciate notes from you that help him or her understand your child's behavior in class. For instance, let the teacher know if your child has recurring stomachaches, is hesitant about coming to school in the morning, has had difficulty with another student at school or

traveling to or from school, or has had a close family member or even a pet die.

It is certainly your perogative to keep your homelife private. But if there is a problem that is occurring or has already occurred, such as divorce, you will find the teacher will be very understanding and sympathetic to your child's needs at this difficult time. He or she can give you valuable input on how your child is handling the situation and whether or not it is affecting schoolwork.

If you are traveling, keep the teacher abreast of your plans. If your child is not going with you, you may want to let the teacher know who will be caring for your child. If your child will be going on the trip also, let the teacher know ahead of time so he or she can send some of the classwork with you.

Keep the lines of communication open. Both you and the teacher want what is best for your child. Whenever you want to meet with your child's teacher, send a note or leave a message at the office, asking when it would be convenient to talk.

TLC FOR TEACHERS

Teachers work hard! There are a variety of things you can do to make the teacher feel appreciated or make his or her job easier. Try one or more of these ideas this year!

Are you baking at home? Send in an extra **cookie** or a piece of pie with your child! This even beats the "apple for the teacher" days! It will make your child feel special also.

Are your roses or other **flowers** blooming? Cut a few for your child to take to school, wrapping the ends in wet paper towels with foil on the outside. What a nice way to brighten up a classroom!

Glue sticks are easier to use than glue bottles with children this age. When students use glue bottles, everything sticks together and there is always a mess! Be a jewel and send your child with a supply of his or her own OR be a real friend and send in a whole box of glue sticks!

Does the teacher have a soft chair? If not, how about providing a small **seat cushion** for him or her to sit on?

Is there a game center in your child's room? Perhaps you could buy an inexpensive **game** to add to the collection, like checkers, magnetic tic-tac-toe, a fun puzzle, or Memory Match.

How is the collection of **books** in your child's classroom? Teachers love to have new literature to read to their students. Check local children's bookstores for suggestions.

If the teacher allows **birthday treats** for your child's birthday, be creative and find something **non-sugary**.

On any given day, let the teacher know that you will provide him or her with **lunch**! You can make it up yourself and deliver it, or purchase something nice from a local restaurant.

A morning **coffee break** can become heaven if you send in apple juice with a bagel and cream cheese.

If you would like to give the teacher a little present at holiday time but are stuck for an idea, try a **gift certificate** at the local educational supply store or bookstore. One to a nearby yogurt shop won't be turned down either!

Don't forget to write **positive little notes** to tell how much your child is enjoying classroom activities and how much you appreciate the teacher!

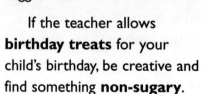

OTHER SCHOOL SERVICES

Your school provides a variety of support services for children beyond the classroom teacher. Become aware of what is available at your school, as well as your district and county. Your child cannot be tested or enrolled in any program without your permission.

School Counselor

Some schools contract with a local agency to have a counselor work with children for a short period of time. A counselor might help children who are having trouble interacting with peers or whose families are going through a divorce, death, or other hardship.

Student Study Teams

Some schools have a Student Study Team which meets once a week. The team may consist of the principal, district psychologist, resource teacher, counselor, and other classroom teachers. If the teacher has a concern about your child, he or she will request your permission to discuss your child with this group. Permission to test your child will be requested if the group feels that would give further clues to any difficulties your child is having. The district psychologist, the resource teacher, or both will administer and share the results of any testing, and you will all jointly determine the best intervention for your child.

Speech Teacher

Several schools may share a speech therapist. He or she will screen students for speech problems and provide pull-out help. If your child needs this type of service, you will be notified and invited to learn more about the program.

Resource Program

Sometimes children have learning handicaps that can be remediated with extra help by specially-trained teachers. Your child may meet with the resource teacher a few days a week for a specified length of time, or the resource teacher may go into your child's classroom and work with individuals or small groups.

Special Education Classes

Placement in Special Education classes can be made for children who are learning disabled, hearing impaired, visually impaired, mentally retarded, or severely emotionally disturbed. These classes may only be at certain schools in your district or county. They are much smaller and generally have a fulltime aide.

Children in Special Education programs may be **mainstreamed** in regular classrooms for part of the day, such as for an art lesson, P.E. class, or science. Other children participate in full **inclusion**, which means they are in a regular classroom all day with the help of their Special Education teacher or aide.

Gifted Program

Gifted programs vary by district. Some have a partial-day or full-day pullout once a week. Others give regular classroom teachers training for challenging gifted children within the class.

TARDIES AND ABSENCES

Tardies

Everyone has mornings that just don't go as planned, but you do not want your child to get into a habit of being tardy. When your child walks in late, it is a disruption to the entire class, makes him or her feel uncomfortable, and starts the day off on the wrong foot.

Schools usually have playground supervision that starts 15–20 minutes before the bell rings. Instead of cutting things close every morning, aim to get your child to the bus stop early or to school when the playground supervision starts. That way when something goes awry, the few minutes spent searching for the missing mitten will not make a difference.

Unplanned Absences

Many schools request that you call in to report a child's absence, while others need a written excuse.

Some want both! If you are not sure which to do, call the school secretary and ask.

If your child has been sick, send a note similar to the following when he or she returns to school:

> Nov. 10, 1998
>
> Dear Mr. Sutter,
>
> Carlos was out of school on November 8th and 9th due to the flu. If he needs to make up any work, please send it home with him.
>
> Sincerely,
>
> Mrs. Garcia

> January 23, 1998
>
> Dear Barbara,
>
> Suzanne will be out of school next week, January 27–30, due to a family trip to Colorado. We want her to keep up with her schoolwork. If you could give Suzanne the assignments ahead of time, we will be sure she completes the work during the trip. Thank you for your time.
>
> Yours truly,
>
> Marie Ste. Germaine

Planned Absences

There may be a time when you know your child is going to be out of school for several days, due to a family trip or other activity.

Notify the office and your child's teacher as much ahead of time as possible. The teacher can provide classwork so your child won't be behind when he or she returns. Also the school cannot collect its ADA money (Average Daily Attendance) for your child unless he or she does the classwork. School districts lose large sums of money when this occurs. To help avoid this be sure to notify the school of any planned absences ahead of time.

Bookmark and Badges

Color in one sunray each time you do your homework without being reminded. Cut center slit. Slip over a button.

I
_____

is a happy "Homework"er!

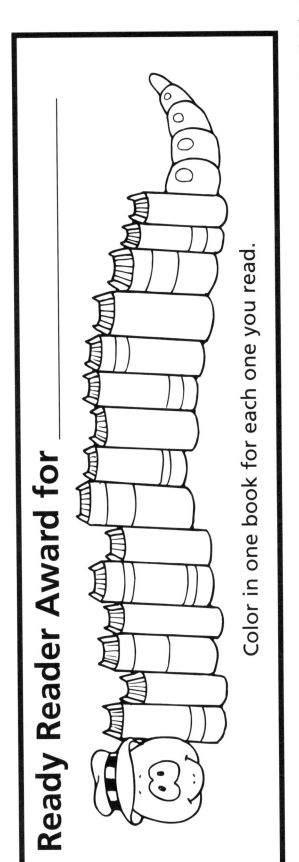

Here I am learning how to _____ !

Paste photo here or cut out this section and let photo show through.

Backs of Rewards

• FS-23003 Skills for Success for Your Second Grader • © Frank Schaffer Publications, Inc.

Vowel Fun

Print the name of each picture on the line.

Short Vowels

--------------- --------------- --------------- ---------------

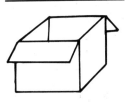 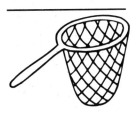 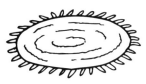 

--------------- --------------- --------------- --------------- ---------------

Long Vowels

A silent **e** at the end of a word makes the first vowel long.

   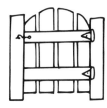

--------------- --------------- --------------- ---------------

Long Vowels

If two vowels go walking, the first one does the talking.

--------------- --------------- --------------- ---------------

Long Vowel Word Box

bike

bone

gate

goat

mule

mail

seal

suit

Phonics Check

Circle the name of each picture.

Consonant Blends

flat
frog
tree

blue
globe
glove

smoke
sled
snake

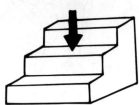
swim
sled
step

flag
slam
free

dress
drum
grape

Consonant Digraphs

ship
shut
chop

chip
shirt
cheese

chimp
thumb
think

what
whale
this

trash
duck
truck

shell
chill
shade

R-Controlled Vowels

farm
ford
fork

barn
bark
burst

park
purse
porch

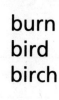
burn
bird
birch

fern
far
first

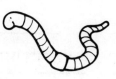
word
work
worm

Sue's Cat

Read the story.

Sue could not find her cat. She looked
in the house. She looked outside. She
still could not find her cat. She asked
Dad to help her. Dad looked under
Sue's bed. Then he looked under the
blankets. No cat!

Just then Sue's brother Ted called,
"I hear something in the garage!"
All of them opened the door to the
garage. There was the cat. She had
a surprise for Sue and Ted and Dad.
New baby kittens!

Circle the answer to each question.

1. Who could not find the cat?
   a. Mom   b. Ted   c. Sue

2. Where did Sue look?
   a. under the bed   b. in the house   c. in the garage

3. Why did Dad look, too?
   a. Sue needed help   b. Ted needed help   c. to find the dog

4. What surprise did the cat have?
   a. a mouse   b. some cheese   c. baby kittens

Bonus! Tell why you think the cat hid.

Can You Answer This?

Do this page after you have read a nonfiction book.

Title _____

Author _____

Book Topic _____

How Can a Fish Fly?

1. In each box write something you learned from the book.

2. Trace the boxes onto another piece of paper.

3. On the new boxes, write a question to match each fact below.

4. Cut out the question boxes. Tape them as a flap to cover the facts.

Tape flap with question here.	Tape flap with question here.
_____ _____ _____ _____	_____ _____ _____ _____
Tape flap with question here.	Tape flap with question here.
_____ _____ _____ _____	_____ _____ _____ _____

Contractions

Draw lines to match the two words and the contraction.

is not •   • haven't   she will •   • we've

have not •   • here's   I am •   • won't

you are •   • isn't   we have •   • let's

he had •   • you're   will not •   • I'm

here is •   • he'd   let us •   • she'll

Write the two words that mean the same as each contraction.

don't _____   I've _____

they're _____   it's _____

wouldn't _____   we'll _____

what's _____   can't _____

Write the contraction for the two words.

I will _____   has not _____

we are _____   she had _____

they have _____

he is _____

could not _____

we have

we've

Bonus! Explain what a contraction is.

Word Endings

Write the base word plus an ending of **s**, **ed**, or **ing**.

play   1. Mark is _____ with Tim.

sleep   2. The baby _____ all night.

walk   3. Anna _____ home last Monday.

climb   4. The dog is _____ the fence!

rain   5. It _____ yesterday.

talk   6. Grandma _____ to us every day.

Write the base word plus the **ed** and **ing** endings.
Remember to double the final consonant.
Example: wag, wagged, wagging

7. tap   _____   _____

8. jog   _____   _____

9. pet   _____   _____

10. grin   _____   _____

Write the base word plus the **ed** and **ing** endings.
Remember to drop the **e** before adding the ending.
Example: chase, chased, chasing

11. hike   _____   _____

12. skate   _____   _____

13. joke   _____   _____

14. bounce   _____   _____

A Handy Plan

Before you start to write, print your subject on the palm of this hand.
On each finger, print an idea about the subject you want to include.

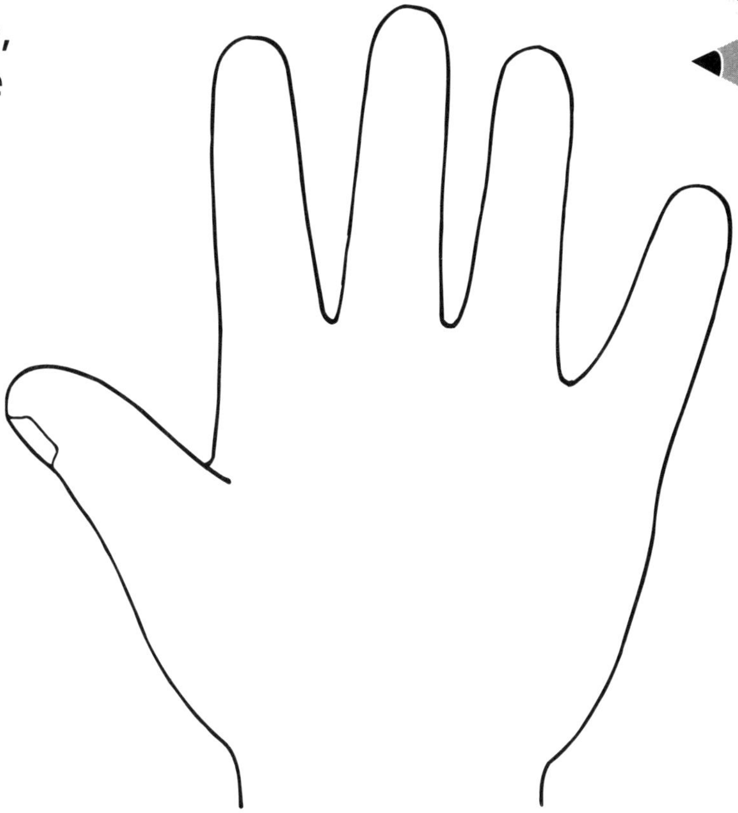

Write a beginning sentence about your subject. Then turn each idea from above into a sentence. Sound out words you don't know how to spell.

_____

_____

_____

_____

_____

_____

_____

_____

Have a parent help you correct what you have written. Rewrite your final copy on another sheet of paper. Color a picture to go with it.

The next time you need a "hand," trace your own to get you started!

A Story Map

Plan a story. Write your ideas below to map it out.

Beginning

Who is the main character?

_____

What is he or she like?

_____

Who else is in the story?

_____

What is he or she like?

_____

Where does the story take place?

_____

_____

When? _____

Middle

What happens?

_____

_____

_____

Then what?

_____

_____

What is the main problem in the story?

_____

_____

End How is the problem solved? _____

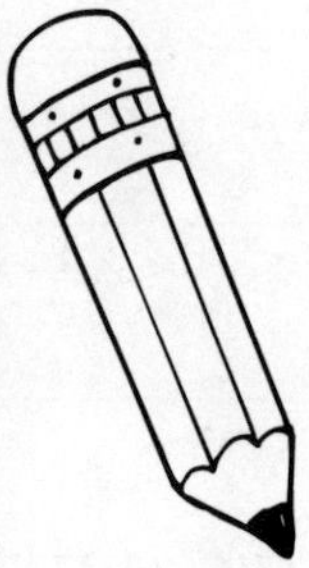

_____

_____

_____

Use your map to write a rough draft of your story. Let a parent help you fix it up. Make a final copy using your best printing. Color a picture to match. You don't need to do this all in one day!

Proofread a Friendly Letter

Circle all letters that need to be capitals.
Write the missing punctuation marks (, or . or ? or !)
where needed. The numbers on the left tell how many
mistakes there are on that line.

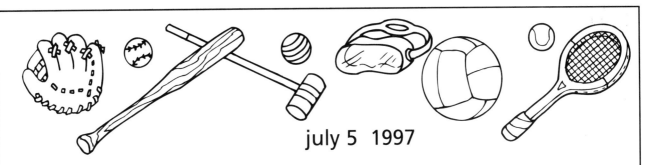

(2)   july 5 1997

(4)   dear grandma and grandpa

(1)   thank you so much for letting me come to visit

(5)   you in june   i really had a super time   the best thing

(4)   we did was visit disneyworld   did you like it, too

(4)   i start school on september 4   i will be in third

(5)   grade   this year my teachers will be mr   ortiz and

(4)   mrs   lawrence

(4)   will you come to see us at thanksgiving   i hope

(3)   so   i love you

(2)   your grandson

(1)   michael

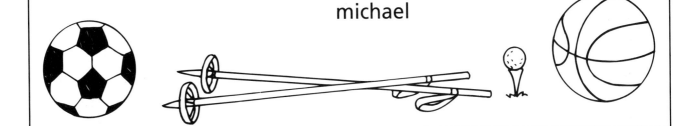

Addition Time

Use any two crayons. In each box, color some of the objects one color, and the rest the other color. Write the two addition sentences to match. Example: 2 + 9 = 11   9 + 2 = 11

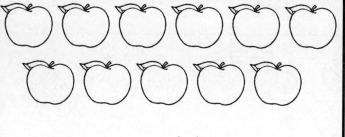

___ + ___ = _11_

___ + ___ = _____

___ + ___ = _12_

___ + ___ = _____

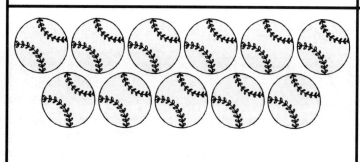

___ + ___ = _____

___ + ___ = _____

___ + ___ = _____

___ + ___ = _____

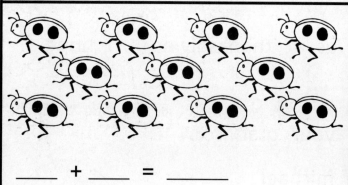

___ + ___ = _____

___ + ___ = _____

___ + ___ = _____

___ + ___ = _____

Use this same idea to learn all of the number combinations of 11, 12, 13, 14, 15, 16, 17, and 18. Make flashcards to go with each.

Subtraction Action

Circle a group in each box. Write the two related subtraction facts.

$17 - 8 = 9$ $17 - 9 = 8$	___ − ___ = ___ ___ − ___ = ___	___ − ___ = ___ ___ − ___ = ___
___ − ___ = ___ ___ − ___ = ___	___ − ___ = ___ ___ − ___ = ___	___ − ___ = ___ ___ − ___ = ___
___ − ___ = ___ ___ − ___ = ___	___ − ___ = ___ ___ − ___ = ___	___ − ___ = ___ ___ − ___ = ___

Bonus! Draw your own boxes with pictures to show more subtraction facts.

Addition Practice

3 + 7 = _____   1 + 9 = _____   6 + 8 = _____

8 + 5 = _____   7 + 6 = _____   9 + 3 = _____

7 + 8 = _____   2 + 9 = _____   6 + 5 = _____

8 + 8 = _____   7 + 5 = _____   9 + 4 = _____

4 + 7 = _____   6 + 4 = _____   6 + 6 = _____

6 + 9 = _____   9 + 9 = _____   4 + 8 = _____

3 + 8 = _____   8 + 9 = _____   5 + 9 = _____

7 + 7 = _____   5 + 5 = _____   9 + 7 = _____

$$\begin{array}{cccccc}
62 & 30 & 52 & 32 & 81 & 30 \\
+\,15 & +\,49 & +\,41 & +\,62 & +\,15 & +\,56
\end{array}$$

$$\begin{array}{cccccc}
70 & 43 & 24 & 47 & 23 & 31 \\
+\,25 & +\,36 & +\,5 & +\,40 & +\,60 & +\,31
\end{array}$$

$$\begin{array}{cccccc}
80 & 40 & 25 & 14 & 32 & 51 \\
+\,1 & +\,24 & +\,73 & +\,71 & +\,13 & +\,8
\end{array}$$

 FS-23003 Skills for Success for Your Second Grader • © Frank Schaffer Publications, Inc.

Subtraction Practice

12 – 5 = _____   18 – 9 = _____   11 – 5 = _____

10 – 3 = _____   15 – 8 = _____   10 – 1 = _____

11 – 7 = _____   14 – 7 = _____   17 – 8 = _____

16 – 9 = _____   12 – 9 = _____   10 – 5 = _____

13 – 5 = _____   11 – 2 = _____   14 – 9 = _____

17 – 9 = _____   13 – 4 = _____   15 – 6 = _____

14 – 8 = _____   10 – 8 = _____   12 – 6 = _____

15 – 7 = _____   16 – 8 = _____   13 – 7 = _____

41	89	53	76	59	46
– 11	– 43	– 32	– 62	– 56	– 30

96	77	69	82	68	49
– 4	– 32	– 57	– 31	– 37	– 21

58	27	82	47	18	69
– 40	– 25	– 10	– 41	– 6	– 14

Regrouping

Add. Look at the ones column first.
Regroup only if you need to.
Think about what you are doing!

9 + 1 = 10

```
  49        38        53        16        26
+ 11      + 53      + 32      + 24      + 49
  60
```

```
  88        67        18        34        76
+  6      + 32      + 77      + 17      + 15
```

```
  16        42        23        53        19
+ 28      + 25      + 27      + 30      + 40
```

Subtract. Look at the ones column first.
Regroup only if you need to.
Think about what you are doing!

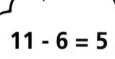

11 - 6 = 5

```
  8
  91        42        88        73        24
- 26      - 19      - 26      - 68      -  8
  65
```

```
  65        77        80        39        52
- 27      - 10      - 57      - 21      - 37
```

```
  48        23        64        51        37
- 36      -  5      - 39      - 28      - 14
```

Word Problems

Write a number sentence to solve each problem. Write the answer.

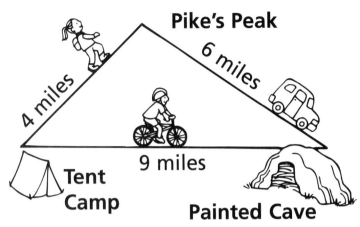

Pike's Peak

4 miles

6 miles

9 miles

Tent Camp

Painted Cave

1. Tom rode his bike from Tent Camp to Painted Cave, and then back to Tent Camp. How many miles did he ride in all?

$$9 \oplus 9 = 18$$

2. Kim and Randy are walking from Tent Camp to Painted Cave. They have gone 3 miles so far. How many more miles do they need to walk?

____ ◯ ____ = ____

3. Bonnie hiked from Tent Camp to Pike's Peak to Painted Cave. How many miles did she hike in all?

____ ◯ ____ = ____

4. Nicole is riding her bike from Painted Cave to Tent Camp. She has 1 more mile to go. How many miles has she ridden so far?

____ ◯ ____ = ____

5. Eric's family drove from Tent Camp to Pike's Peak, to Painted Cave, and back to Tent Camp. How many miles did they drive?

____ ◯ ____ ◯ ____ = ____

Dimes and Pennies

Count the dimes and pennies. Write how many cents.

1.

Dimes	Pennies
4	2

4 2 ¢

2.

Dimes	Pennies

_____

3.

Dimes	Pennies

_____

4.

Dimes	Pennies

_____

5.

Dimes	Pennies

_____

6.

Dimes	Pennies

_____

7.

Dimes	Pennies

_____

8.

Dimes	Pennies

_____

 FS-23003 Skills for Success for Your Second Grader • © Frank Schaffer Publications, Inc.

Hundreds, Tens, Ones

Write how many hundreds (H), tens (T), and ones (O).
Then write the number in the basket.

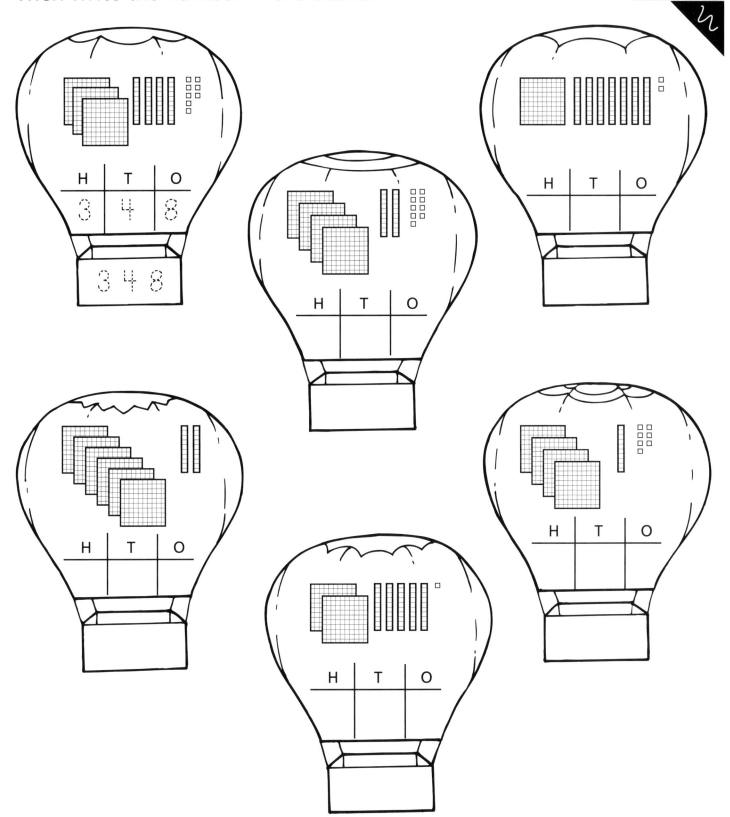

Metric Measuring

Estimate the length in centimeters (cm)
of each mouse's path to the cheese.
Then use a centimeter ruler to measure it.

	My Estimate	Actual Length
a.	___ cm	___ cm
b.	___ cm	___ cm
c.	___ cm	___ cm
d.	___ cm	___ cm
e.	___ cm	___ cm
f.	___ cm	___ cm
g.	___ cm	___ cm
h.	___ cm	___ cm

Use this centimeter ruler if you don't have one.

```
 1  2  3  4  5  6  7  8  9  10  11  12  13  14  15  16
Centimeters (cm)
```

Reading a Calendar

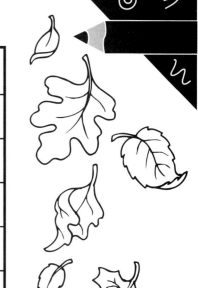

Fill in the missing numbers.

SEPTEMBER						
Sun.	Mon.	Tues.	Wed.	Thurs.	Fri.	Sat.
	1	2			5	
7	8					13
		16		18		
			24			
		30				

1. How many Mondays are there in September? _____

   List the dates that fall on Mondays. _____

2. How many Fridays are there in September? _____

   List the dates that fall on Fridays. _____

3. What is the date of these September days?

   a. first Sunday _____   d. fourth Saturday _____

   b. third Wednesday _____   e. fifth Tuesday _____

   c. second Thursday _____   f. first Monday _____

Science Investigations

1. I want to learn more about this topic:

_____

2. This is what I already know about the topic:

_____

_____

_____

3. This is what I want to learn:

_____

_____

_____

4. This is how I could learn more:

_____

_____

_____

5. Here's what I did learn!

_____

_____

_____

_____

Animal Groups

Color the correct animals for each category.
Cross out the one that doesn't belong.
Write the name of another animal for each group.

Birds

_____

Fish

_____

Mammals

_____

Insects

_____

Reptiles

_____

Grandparent Interview

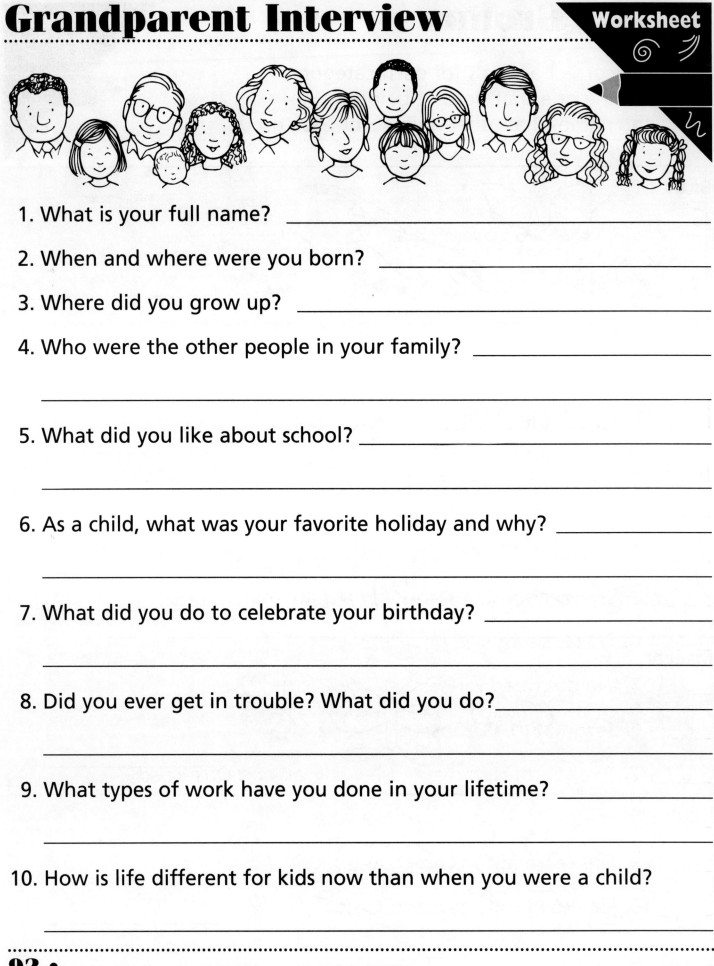

1. What is your full name? _____

2. When and where were you born? _____

3. Where did you grow up? _____

4. Who were the other people in your family? _____

   _____

5. What did you like about school? _____

   _____

6. As a child, what was your favorite holiday and why? _____

   _____

7. What did you do to celebrate your birthday? _____

   _____

8. Did you ever get in trouble? What did you do? _____

   _____

9. What types of work have you done in your lifetime? _____

   _____

10. How is life different for kids now than when you were a child?

    _____

Reading a Map

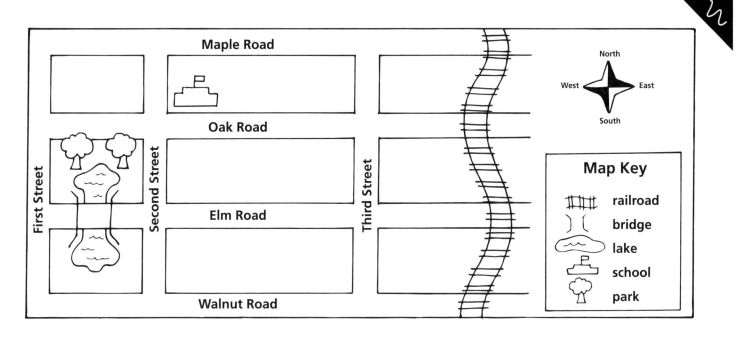

Read the map. Write **T** if the sentence is true or **F** if it is false.

_____ 1. Maple Road is on the north end of town.

_____ 2. First Street is east of Third Street.

_____ 3. The symbol ⊞⊞ stands for a railroad.

_____ 4. There is a bridge on Elm Road.

_____ 5. Walnut Road is north of Oak Road.

_____ 6. Second Street is west of the park.

_____ 7. The school is between Maple Road and Oak Road.

_____ 8. Maple Road goes over the lake.

_____ 9. The railroad runs north and south.

_____ 10. Elm Road runs east and west.

What Are Your Physical Skills?

Fill this in at the beginning of the year and then at the end of the year.

	Beginning of the year	End of the year
1. For how many minutes can you walk without stopping?	_____ minutes	_____ minutes
2. For how many minutes can you run without stopping?	_____ minutes	_____ minutes
3. How many times can you hop on your left foot?	_____ times	_____ times
4. How many times can you hop on your right foot?	_____ times	_____ times
5. How many times can you jump rope without missing?	_____ times	_____ times
6. How well can you throw a ball? (not so well, OK, very well)	_____	_____
7. How well can you catch a ball? (not so well, OK, very well)	_____	_____
8. How well can you bounce a ball? (not so well, OK, very well)	_____	_____
9. How well can you kick a ball? (not so well, OK, very well)	_____	_____
10. How often are you a good sport? (never, sometimes, usually, always)	_____	_____

 FS-23003 Skills for Success for Your Second Grader • © Frank Schaffer Publications, Inc.